The Legislan

**THE
REGENTS
PRESS
OF KANSAS**

*takes pleasure in
sending you this copy
for review*

Price

$11.50

Publication Date

February 26, 1979

*Two clippings of your review
will be appreciated*

366 WATSON LIBRARY
LAWRENCE, KANSAS 660-45

Arizona State Univ.
West Campus Library

The Legislature as an Organization

A Study of the Kansas Legislature

A15040 425590

by

Marvin A. Harder and Raymond G. Davis

with the assistance of
Steven Carter and Louis Chabira

JK
6871
.H37
West

THE REGENTS PRESS OF KANSAS
Lawrence

Arizona State Univ.
West Campus Library

© Copyright 1979 by The Regents Press of Kansas
Printed in the United States of America

Library of Congress Cataloging in Publication Data

Harder, Marvin Andrew, 1921–
The legislature as an organization.

Bibliography: p.
Includes index.
1. Kansas. Legislature. I. Davis, Raymond G.,
1941–   joint author. II. Title.
JK6871.H37   328.781   78-25721
ISBN 0-7006-0187-2

Contents

Preface   vii

1 The Tools of Analysis   1

2 The Participants   7

3 The Committees   29

4 Lawmaking: The Dominant Technology   41

5 Overseeing: The Emerging Technology   61

6 The Role of Leadership:
Managing the Technologies   81

7 Legislative Staff   95

8 Networks of Communication
and Socialization   109

9 Change in the Kansas Legislature   137

10 Assessment   163

Notes   173

Index   181

Preface

A legislature is an *organization* and, as such, makes decisions quite similar to those which are made in all modern corporations:

1. It divides labor, assigning special tasks to particular units.
2. It develops technologies, ways and means of converting inputs into outputs.
3. It assigns managerial responsibilities to particular positions.
4. It recruits personnel to perform designated tasks.
5. It maintains an incentive system to encourage productivity and the stability of its work force.
6. It acquires and maintains facilities and equipment to meet organizational needs.
7. It seeks to protect its technologies from certain kinds of outside influences.
8. It trains its personnel to enhance job performance.
9. It budgets its resources, decreasing and increasing expenditures from year to year.
10. It assesses its structure and procedures from time to time.
11. It evaluates its outputs.
12. It is concerned with its public image and takes steps periodically to improve it.

Though it can be argued that the analogy is strained, that the similarities between a private manufacturing enterprise and a state legislature are superficial, and that the bottom line in corporate decision-making—namely, profits—is fundamentally dissimilar from the bottom line of legislative decision-making—namely, reelection—it can also be argued that no one who really wishes to unravel the complexities of a legislature can succeed without attending to its organizational characteristics. The latter argument stimulated the writing of this book. This is a descriptive and critical analysis of the Kansas legislature, written from the perspective of organization theory.

In 1971 the American Political Science Association sought foundation funding for the State Legislative Service Program. The principals made the case for materials that could assist and encourage orientation sessions, and they proposed that political scientists be commissioned to prepare legislative manuals. The program was funded by the Ford Foundation, and scholars in many states were designated to undertake the analytical tasks of describing legislative procedures.

In Kansas, the State Legislative Service Project resulted in a book about the Kansas legislature which was not a manual but a treatise written from the perspectives familiar to political scientists. In time it became evident that *The Kansas Legislature*, written by Marvin Harder and Carolyn Rampey (Lawrence: University Press of Kansas, 1972), had not addressed certain questions about legislative decision-making. What was needed was a companion book that would focus on organizational processes.

During the spring of 1976 the Legislative Coordinating Council authorized the second Institute for Kansas Legislators and directed Dr. Marvin Harder to plan the program. With the advice and consent of the Speaker of the House of Representatives, Duane S. McGill, it was decided that background papers helpful to the assessment of legislative procedure and the roles of leaders and staff should be prepared for the institute.

With the assistance of Steve Carter (administrative assistant to the Speaker), Louis Chabira, James Murphy, and Judith McConnell, daily meetings of the House of Representatives and several standing committees were observed, and journals were prepared during the 1976 session. After the session ended, Dr. Harder met with this group in the Speaker's office each week for the purpose of sharing insights and exploring strategies for developing papers from the institute. The group was joined in these meetings by James Weber, a graduate assistant from the Institute of Social and Environmental Studies of the University of Kansas. These conversations led to the decision to explore organization theory in order to discover a perspective and tools of analysis.

In late summer, Dr. Raymond Davis agreed to prepare a paper on "The Institutionalization of the Kansas Legislature" and, with Dr. Harder, to coauthor a manuscript for publication, which would represent a look at the Kansas legislature from the perspective of organization theory and which would utilize both the materials prepared for the institute and the proceedings of the institute. Professor Davis had written his doctoral dissertation on organization theory and had served as a member of the staff of the California legislature before he joined the faculty of political science at the University of Kansas. Steven Carter and Louis Chabira were asked to prepare papers on "Legislative Leadership" and "Networks of Communications and Socialization," respectively.

The first drafts of background papers for the institute were reviewed by senior staff members of the legislature, including Phillip Jones, Richard Ryan, and Marlin Rein of the Legislative Research Department; Fred Carmen, Arden Ensley, and Norman Furse of the Revisor of Statutes Office; Dr. Richard Brown, director of the Legislative Post Audit Division; and William Bachman, director of Legislative Administrative Services. They provided information, identified inaccuracies in the drafts, and suggested additions that substantially improved the papers.

The first and subsequent drafts of the book were read by Phillip Jones and Richard Ryan. Their willingness to share their special knowledge and to devote time to reading provided a model that the professional authors may hope to emulate when they read student papers.

The decision to write a book based on the preparatory work for the institute represented a second purpose. Both Dr. Davis and Dr. Harder had concluded that a modest contribution to the scholarly literature on state legislatures and the legislative process might be accomplished, because relatively little attention had been given by political scientists to organization theory as an analytical approach. This volume is the result of their collaboration.

The authors are greatly indebted to the leaders and members of the Kansas legislature, to the senior staff members, and to their colleagues for their thoughts and encouragement. They are particularly indebted to Speaker McGill, who shared with Dr. Harder his insights and information and who was the constant and vigorous supporter of the Institute for Kansas Legislators.

Reba Cobb, a graduate student in public administration at the University of Kansas, provided the authors with research assistance during the time the manuscript was in preparation. Barbara Watkins edited copy, eliminating redundancies and improving sentence structure and punctuation. Our colleague Professor Brinton Milward read the entire manuscript, utilizing his considerable knowledge of organization theory as a basis for his criticisms. Lisa Berry and Joan Nickum contributed many hours to typing various drafts of every chapter. The compensation these people received was much less than they deserved.

Research and editing costs were funded by grants from the Research Committee of the University of Kansas and the Intergovernmental Personnel Act, administered by the United States Civil Service Commission (in Kansas, by the Division of Personnel of the State Department of Administration), and from legislative appropriations for the Institute for Kansas Legislators and the Capitol Complex Center of the University of Kansas.

The authors are indebted to Professors Malcolm Jewell of the University of Kentucky and Alan Rosenthal of the Eagleton Institute of Politics and to their colleague Dennis Palumbo, for reading all or parts of the manuscript. Their suggestions were helpful in the revisions of the manuscript.

Finally, the authors acknowledge their special intellectual debt to James Thompson, author of *Organizations in Action*, whose delineations of the main concepts used in this study were helpful throughout the writing. With all of these debts, the shortcomings remain the authors' responsibility.

Marvin Harder
Raymond G. Davis

Lawrence, Kansas
January 1978

1

The Tools of Analysis

Most political scientists, journalists, and legislators who have studied and written about the Congress of the United States and/or state legislatures have engaged in *political* analysis. That is, they have treated legislatures as arenas in which interests of various kinds compete to influence decision-making, and they have assumed that the central task of analysis is to identify the forms and conditions of influence. To the end of explaining decisions and nondecisions they have fashioned and employed concepts, or tools of analysis, such as access, bargaining, constituency, blocs, informal groups, style, and institutionalization. And they have utilized such familiar concepts as power, persuasion, interest groups, leadership, public opinion, partisanship, and voting. All these concepts have become the currency of communications among those who have been interested and attentive to the activities of American legislative bodies as well as to American politics generally.

Organizational analysts have generated another body of literature and a special vocabulary. The sociologists, psychologists, economists, and scholars in public and business administration, while utilizing many of the terms employed in political analyses, have constructed conceptual tools appropriate to their needs. Over time, new and borrowed concepts appeared in their writings as the focus was enlarged to include organizations' interactions with and linkages to the market-place, or the environment, as well as the formal distribution of authority within organizations and the ways in which work is planned, assigned, performed, coordinated, and supervised. Today, it is appropriate to describe organization theory as bounded by an interest in intra- and interorganizational behavior. From this literature the authors of this book have selected certain concepts that they believe to be helpful in understanding the Kansas legislature as an organization.

In a relative sense, the organizational characteristics of legislatures have been neglected by both political and organizational analysts. The former, influenced by the perspective called behavioralism, have tended to minimize the importance of organizational structure and procedure in explaining patterns of influence. The latter have concentrated their efforts toward understanding private and public organizations commonly thought of as being bureaucratic. The result has been a paucity of information in scholarly literature about the organizational aspects of American state legislatures.[1]

The dearth of studies about legislative organization posed an intellectual challenge to the authors, an incentive that was reinforced by the need of freshmen legislators in Kansas for a structural and procedural description of the institution to which they have been elected and by the need of all Kansas legislators for an analysis and critique that would be helpful in the process of organizational assessment.

Some members of both potential groups of readers, scholars and Kansas legislators, are likely to be troubled by the meaning of certain concepts derived from organization theory that are used throughout this book. To assist understanding, a glossary follows. The brief statements of meaning are presented in approximately the order in which they are first used. Some of the terms will be defined again in certain chapters to remind the reader of their meanings.

Task environment. Every organization is affected by the activities of individuals and groups who are not members, and most organizations are more directly affected by some "outsiders" than by others. Those groups that can and do influence the setting and attaining of the goals of an organization constitute the task environment. Where that influence is recognized and accepted as a "fact of life," a condition of dependency may be said to exist. For example, community welfare organizations that derive most of their funds from allocations of a central fund-raising agency (for example, the Community Chest) would perceive that agency's decisions as being important to their operations. To the extent that the allocating agency could increase, decrease, or even deny funds entirely, the welfare organizations would perceive their condition as one of dependence. They could hardly make decisions about the setting and attainment of goals without considering the policies and procedures of the allocating agency. In this illustration, the allocating agency is a part of the task environment of all community welfare organizations. Other organizations in a community might directly or indirectly affect citizen attitudes toward community welfare programs, and thus affect the environment in which the welfare organizations carry on their work, but usually their effects would be too indirect to justify their inclusion in the category of task environment.

Technology. Organizations are created in order to achieve one or more goals. Those who bring an organization into being and those who subsequently manage it design means of accomplishing each purpose. Means (ways, processes, procedures) that are consciously developed are called technologies. The mass-production line symbolizes technology for many. The computerized system of controlling rockets in space symbolizes technology for others. But the concept of technology is not limited to the conversion or control of physical matter. Any rational process by which an organization converts inputs (whatever they may be) into outputs (including both intangibles, such as ideas, and tangibles, such as houses) is a technology.

The technology of an organization affects its structure. The assignment and grouping of tasks and the manner in which work is supervised and coordinated—that is, elements of structure—will be greatly influenced, if not determined, by the technology. A parts department in a manufacturing organization exists because it is considered necessary to the operation of the manufacturing technology. By the same token, the structure of a legislative organization is affected by the law-making technology.

Buffering. James Thompson explains buffering as follows:

> To maximize productivity of a manufacturing technology, the technical core must be able to operate as if the market will absorb the single kind of product at a continuous rate, and as if inputs flowed continuously, at a steady rate and with specified quality. Conceivably both sets of conditions could occur; realistically they do not. But or-

ganizations reveal a variety of devices for approximating these "as if" assumptions, with input and output components meeting fluctuating environments and converting them into steady conditions for the technological core.[2]

A legislature buffers its lawmaking technology from the uncertainties that accompany reliance on the executive branch and on interest groups for its agenda, that is, for the inputs (proposals) it converts into outputs (decisions). The ability of a legislature to satisfy citizen demands for the resolution of public problems is perceived as requiring the formulations of appropriate proposals. The interim committee system of the Kansas legislature, which is designed to study problems and to develop or evaluate proposals, may therefore be thought of as a buffering device.

The term "buffering" will also be used to describe certain rules that limit access of outsiders to legislators at certain stages in the lawmaking process. This usage is only a slight deviation from Thompson's meaning of the term. If, for example, lobbyists and citizens generally are prohibited from walking into a chamber during a session, that prohibition may be viewed as a means of protecting the lawmaking technology from potential disruptions. The fact that individual lawmakers may perceive the rule as giving them a freedom from overt pressure at certain moments does not contradict the idea that the rule may serve the organizational need to maintain an orderly and expeditious process of lawmaking.

Institutions and institutional imperatives. Those who are attentive to what legislators say in their campaigns and in dialogues and debates in committee rooms and on the floors of the House and Senate may discover that legislators make explicit what the public expects of the legislature. These expectations, taken together, explain what is meant by the statement that the legislature is an *institution.* An institution is an organization with a *public* consisting of citizens who share certain general understandings of what services should be performed. Because these expectations remain constant and because they are constraining, a legislature exhibits stability and uniformity, notwithstanding the fact that the turnover of membership may be relatively high.

Consider the following as a partial list of public expectations, beliefs that both guide and limit legislative behavior:

1. The legislature should enact general laws, laws that are equally applicable to all persons who belong to a class.

2. The legislature should enact laws that resolve or manage problems that citizens cannot cope with individually.

3. The legislature should respect the constitution by honoring its mandates and limitations.

4. The legislature should be open and accessible to citizens who wish to petition for or against proposed legislation.

5. The legislature should be prudent in the allocation of tax revenues.

6. The legislature should avoid becoming dominated by any special-interest group or combination of interest groups.

7. The legislature should proceed with its business in an orderly manner.

8. The legislature should make known the content of its deliberations and decisions.

9. The legislature should act as a check upon the activities of both the executive and the judicial branches of government.

Though judgments vary from session to session about how faithfully a legislature has lived up to these precepts, as judgments also vary about how attentive the public is to what legislators do and do not do, no one questions the assumption that the legislature risks public censure if its actions appear to ignore or violate the public's expectations. These risks are made real by the fact that legislators cannot continue to hold their positions unless they win elections every two or four years.

The contrast between organizations in the public and private sectors that are institutions and those that are not is heightened by the realization that noninstitutional organizations are relatively freer than institutional organizations in making decisions about what they will do and will not do and how they will do what they choose to do. Though every organization must adjust to certain environmental constraints, the latitude in decision-making that is enjoyed by noninstitutional organizations is greater than that enjoyed by institutional organizations.

Philip Selznick has employed the distinction between organization and institution in analyzing the demands placed on leaders. In rough form, his argument is that leaders of institutions must look outward as well as inward, that they are faced with a duality of roles.[3] Selznick's application of the concept of "institution" is borrowed in the chapter on the role of leadership.

Uncertainty. The word "uncertainty" is so common and unambiguous that a definition would not seem to be necessary. But because uncertainty is "the fundamental problem of complex organizations" and coping with uncertainty is "the essence of the administrative process"[4] and because the term will be used frequently in this book, it is essential that its meaning in the context of organization theory be made explicit.

Much of the activity that now occurs in complex private and public organizations would not occur if cause/effect relationships were understood. If tomorrow's legislators could know precisely what causes certain public problems and could also know how certain actions would affect those causal conditions, it is highly probable that the lawmaking technology would be changed substantially. No one speculates about those possible or probable changes because no one believes such certainties to be imminent. Uncertainties, rather than certainties, are, in general, the condition of the environment in which legislative organizations function. That seemingly elemental fact is the key to understanding much of what happens and doesn't happen in legislative organizations (or so the authors will argue).

Except for the concepts defined above, this organizational study of the Kansas legislature is relatively free of technical terminology. And, we hope, it is also free of pretentious language. The next two chapters are threaded by a familiar idea that has long been associated with the word "organization," and that is the specialization of tasks.

2
The Participants

No other organization in society in toto approximates a state legislature. Any analogy is in some way misleading, or worse, an invidious comparison. One could say, for example, that a legislature is like a cannery in the sense that many of its employees are seasonal. It is like a college in that its principals formulate, assemble, and present ideas. It is like a church in its adherence to ritual. And it is like a political party in the diversity of its membership. But all these comparisons are strained. None captures the ethos of a legislature. Even city councils and school boards, which are sometimes called legislative bodies, are similar only in their policy-making function and in the fact that the members are elected to their positions. The bicameral structure, the ritualized technologies of making laws and overseeing the operations of the executive branch, the complicated networks of communications, and the large number of participants, both members and nonmembers—all make legislatures a unique kind of organization.

Since all these attributes are distinguishing characteristics, there is no logical point of departure for a descriptive-analytical study of a legislative organization. The authors have chosen to begin by examining the payroll of the Kansas legislature; more specifically, the numbers of employees by job categories. Though categorization con-

7

ceals the myriad of personality differences in an organization as large as a state legislature, categories bring into bold relief the essence of all organizations, and that is the specialization of tasks by which people pursue goals and objectives that cannot be achieved otherwise.

In 1977 there were 516 men and women who were part-time or full-time employees of the Kansas legislature. By employees we mean persons who receive compensation from funds appropriated for the maintenance of the legislature. Included are legislators; excluded are those who may be remunerated for consulting services. By numbers of employees the Kansas legislature ranks in the top 2 percent of organizations in the state of Kansas.[1] The legislature is by no means the largest public organization in the state. The Department of Social and Rehabilitation Services employed 2,400 Kansans in 1977.

Though legislative employees are not a part of the civil-service system in Kansas, all positions are labeled, and there is a rough correspondence between the description of a position and the salary. Table 2.1 lists all the classifications by suborganization. Assuming that the work performed by individuals is similar by category and that most full-time employees are relatively secure in their jobs, it is appropriate to think of the legislature as an organization having its own personnel system.

The total number of legislative employees (516) drops precipitously at the end of each session. Exclusive of legislators, many of whom serve on interim committees that meet on call of the chairmen, only 129, or 36 percent of the total, can be considered full-time employees.

The position titles listed in table 2.1, taken together, suggest the kinds of tasks performed in a legislative organization, but they are not very helpful as indicators of responsibility or competencies required in the performance of the legislature's dominant technology—namely, lawmaking—nor do they reveal the kinds of expertise that individuals acquire over time. A typology, based on these criteria, that brings us a step closer to this level of understanding is one that divides the personnel into (1) legislators, (2) administrators, (3) professionals, (4) clerks and secretaries, and (5) retainers. Table 2.2 identifies the number of employees who belong to each category.

Though all the duties performed by personnel in all five categories are essential in the life of a legislature, the order in which the categories are listed in table 2.2 is consistent with the degree to which the persons in each category are responsible for the performance of a

TABLE 2.1

TITLES OF POSITIONS AND NUMBERS OF LEGISLATIVE EMPLOYEES BY UNIT, 1977

Unit	Title of Position	Number
Legislators	Senate	40
	House of Representatives	125
Legislative Research Department	Director	1
	Associate director	1
	Chief fiscal analyst	1
	Research associate	3
	Principal analyst	5
	Research analyst	2
	Research assistant	5
	Fiscal analyst	6
	Office manager	1
	Secretary	2
	Clerk III	1
	Clerk-typist II	3
Revisor of Statutes	Revisor of statutes	1
	First assistant revisor	1
	Senior assistant revisor	1
	Assistant revisor	8
	Editor of statutes	1
	Assistant editor of statutes	1
	Secretary	9
	Computer technician	2
	Law clerk	4
Legislative Post Audit	Post auditor	1
	Deputy post auditor	1
	Assistant post auditor	1
	Director of audit	2
	Audit manager	3
	Principal auditor	1
	Senior auditor	4
	Auditor	10
	Associate auditor	9½
	Administrative associate	1
	Coordinator of publications	1
	Office manager	1
	Senior typist	1
	Typist	2
	Clerk	1½

TABLE 2.1 (continued)
TITLES OF POSITIONS AND NUMBERS OF LEGISLATIVE EMPLOYEES BY UNIT, 1977

Unit	Title of Position	Number
Legislative Administrative Services*	Director	1
	Secretary of the Senate	1
	Chief clerk of the House	1
	Assistant secretary of the Senate	1
	Assistant chief clerk	1
	Administrative assistant	9
	Sergeant at arms	6
	Chaplain	2
	Doorkeeper	17
	Supply officer	1
	Historian	2
	Journal clerk	9
	Bill clerk	3
	Calendar clerk	4
	Docket clerk	2
	Enrolling clerk	3
	Reading clerk	2
	Proof reader	1
	Messenger	3
	Postmaster	1
	Postal clerk	3
	Document clerk	16
	Information clerk	3
	Page clerk	2
	Messenger	2
	Secretary†	125
	File clerk	30
Legislative Counsel	Legislative counsel	1
	Secretary	1

* The positions listed in this category are not in hierarchical order. Those who exercise primary supervisory responsibilities include the director, the secretary of the Senate, the clerk of the House, chief sergeants at arms, chief clerk of the Documents Room, and the postmaster.
† Secretarial positions include secretaries to legislative leaders, committees, and desk staffs.

TABLE 2.2

NUMBERS OF PARTICIPANTS, BY RESPONSIBILITIES AND SKILLS

Category	Number
Legislators	165
Administrators	11
Professionals	67*
Clerks and secretaries	250
Retainers	23

* Does not include administrators who are also professionals.

legislature's functions. Some of the differences in performances within each classification will be explored in the sections that follow.

LEGISLATORS

The citizen-legislators in Kansas are a heterogeneous group. Their critics might prefer a pejorative description such as the Shakespearean phrase "a motley crew" or a "caboodle," meaning an unassorted collection. The deprecating of state legislators—and, more recently, of members of Congress—has been a favorite pastime of political wags throughout American history. Perhaps the diversity of the citizen's elected representatives invites caricature of the group, because there are always a few who behave ludicrously on occasion.

But such stereotypes lose their credibility when legislators are observed in their organizational environment. They are perceived as the decision-makers, each of whom participates in most phases of the lawmaking process and some of whom are active in every phase. The observable differences among legislators are in the energy that they expend, the satisfaction that they derive from their participation, and the influence that they exert. While not precisely measurable, these differences seem to affect organizational performance. Those who are energetic and enjoy their work appear to be the most influential generally. Certain outputs of the legislature are seen as results of the configuration of the primary interests of the influential legislators.

In the well-known work *The Lawmakers*,[2] James David Barber labeled the influential legislators as the "lawmakers." In his typology the lawmakers are distinguishable from spectators, advertisers, and "reluctants." Spectators are low in activity but high in willingness to return, and they contribute to the reduction of tension. Advertisers are high in activity but low in willingness to return, and they generally have a negative effect on organizational morale. Reluctants are low in activity and low in willingness to return, but they help maintain important legislative norms. Lawmakers are high in activity and high in willingness to return, and they make the most significant contributions. They do so, argues Barber, because there is a congruence between their personal strategies and the tasks that a legislature requires of legislators.

A similar study of the personnel of complex organizations, private as well as public, might reveal similar personality types. Robert Presthus suggested the universality of such differences in his book *The Organizational Society*.[3] He typed personalities in bureaucratic structures as "upward-mobiles," "ambivalents," and "indifferents." The upward-mobiles are those who are willing to conform to organizational norms in order to obtain the rewards that the organizations dispense. The ambivalents are those who want the rewards but are unwilling to live within the constraints of expectations. Finally, the indifferents are those who do what they must but are not motivated by the incentives that the organization offers.

A legislature differs from many organizations in the private and public sectors in the relative inattention given by legislatures to development of an incentive system. Incentives in legislatures are taken as givens. Generally speaking, few within the legislature care whether individual legislators choose to seek reelection. The organization will have a full complement of legislators in any case, and the products of legislative work are perceived as not likely to be affected by who participates and who does not. That observation may be an overstatement, but it serves to underscore a characteristic of a legislative organization that makes it rather unlike other organizations in which high turnover is believed to contribute to organizational inefficiency.[4]

But there are legislators and students of the legislative process who believe that state legislatures suffer from the lack of legislator expertise in functional areas, the level of knowledge that members of Congress acquire by long, continued service on a committee. Some United States senators and representatives become as expert in certain subject matters as the experts whom they call to testify. If it is true, as it seems to be, that continued service on a committee is a process of continuing education, then it is difficult for the Kansas legislature to acquire in-house legislator expertise. The average length of service of

TABLE 2.3

NUMBER OF TERMS SERVED BY KANSAS STATE SENATORS AND REPRESENTATIVES,
1977

Senate

Name	Number of Terms	Name	Number of Terms
Donald L. Allegruci	1	Mike Johnston	1
Charlie L. Angell	2	Fred A. Kerr	1
Neil H. Arasmith	2	Billy Q. McCray	2
Arnold Berman	1	Jan Meyers	2
Paul Burke	1	Bill Morris	1
John E. Chandler	1	William Mulich	2
Bert Chaney	2	Joseph F. Norwell	1
John W. Crofoot	3	Jim Parrish	2
Ross O. Doyen	3	Elwaine F. Pomeroy	3
Donn J. Everett	1	Tom Rehorn	1
Paul Feleciano, Jr.	1	Edward F. Reilly	4
James L. Francisco	2	Larry J. Rogers	1
Norman E. Gaar	4	John M. Simpson	3
Franklin D. Gaines	2	Frank Smith	1
Richard G. Gannon	1	Wesley H. Sowers	3
Joseph C. Harder	5	Jack Steineger	5
Leroy A. Hayden	1	Robert V. Talkington	2
Ronald R. Hein	1	John F. Vermillion	3
Paul Hess	2	Joe Warren	6
Jack W. Janssen	4	Wint Winter	4

Average: 2.2 terms (8.8 years)

House

Name	Number of Terms	Name	Number of Terms
Richard D. Adams	1	Michael G. Johnson	2
Arnold R. Anderson	2	Mrs. Harold Jones	4
Geneva J. Anderson	2	Norman E. Justice	3
R. E. Arbuthnot	4	Victor W. Kearns	3
Patrick D. Augustine	1	Wendell E. Lady	5
Douglas L. Baker	1	Charles F. Laird	3
William M. Beezley	1	Robin Dee Leach	1
August Bogina, Jr.	2	J. B. Littlejohn	1
James D. Braden	2	Marvin L. Littlejohn	2
E. Richard Brewster	2	C. Fred Lorentz	2

TABLE 2.3 (continued)

NUMBER OF TERMS SERVED BY KANSAS STATE SENATORS AND REPRESENTATIVES, 1977

House (continued)			
Name	*Number of Terms*	*Name*	*Number of Terms*
William W. Bunten	8	Clarence C. Love	6
Denny D. Burgess	3	James E. Lowther	1
Ralph E. Bussman	2	Ruth Luzzati	3
Lloyd D. Buzzi	3	R. D. McCrum	2
Robert C. Caldwell	1	Donald E. Mainey	3
Clifford V. Campbell	2	John J. Maloney	1
John Carlin	4	Phil Martin	1
Gerald Caywood	1	Ardena Matlack	2
Carlos M. Cooper	4	Mike Meacham	1
Theo Cribbs	3	Joseph M. Mikesic	14
Rex Crowell	2	Robert H. Miller	4
Don E. Crumbaker	4	O. Mills	3
James Cubit	11	John M. Modrcin	1
Ambrose L. Dempsey	12	W. Edgar Moore	3
Arden Dierdorff	10	Anita G. Niles	2
Herman G. Dillon	1	Irving R. Niles	8
Arthur Douville	2	Belva J. Ott (apptd.)	1
J. Sanford Duncan	3	Alva Lee Powell	6
Harold P. Dyck	4	William J. Reardon	2
William M. Eddy	1	John H. Reimer	1
Roy M. Ehrlich	4	Roger R. Robertson	3
Larry E. Erne	1	Jack L. Rodrock	2
Keith Farrar	3	Pascal Allen Roniger	5
Ward P. Ferguson	1	Fred W. Rosenau	6
Ben Foster	4	Kent Roth	1
Kenneth Francisco	2	Ivan Sand	1
Robert G. Frey	2	Richard R. Schmidt	1
Leroy F. Fry	1	Charles J. Schwartz	1
Roy H. Garrett	5	E. Dean Shelor	1
Eugene F. Gastl	6	John F. Shriver	1
Stan Gibson	1	Burr Sifers	1
Michael G. Glover	3	Jim Slattery	3
Francis Gordon	1	Tom Slattery	2
James H. Guffey	1	John F. Stites	1
Lee Hamm	3	Kathryn Sughrue	1
Richard L. Harper	7	John F. Sutter	4

TABLE 2.3 (concluded)
NUMBER OF TERMS SERVED BY KANSAS STATE SENATORS AND REPRESENTATIVES,
1977

	House (continued)		
Name	*Number of Terms*	*Name*	*Number of Terms*
Mike Hayden	3	J. E. Talley	1
John F. Hayes	7	Dan Thiessen	5
David John Heinemann	5	Marjorie J. Thomson	1
Robert C. Henry	1	Larry F. Turnquist	1
Anthony Hensley	1	James L. Ungerer	5
Sharon Hess	2	John H. Vogel	8
Kalo A. Hineman	2	Richard Walker	3
Dean B. Hinshaw	1	Fred L. Weaver	4
Joseph Hoagland	3	Darrel M. Webb	1
John L. Hodges	1	Neal D. Whitaker	3
Loren H. Hohman	2	Lynn W. Whiteside	4
James Holderman	5	Robert Whittaker	2
Tim Holt	1	Ruth W. Wilkin	3
Rex B. Hoy	5	George Wingert	4
Patrick J. Hurley	2	Bill Wisdom	2
John T. Ivy	3	George H. Works	3
Homer E. Jarchow	1		

Average: 3.0 terms (5.8 years)

a Kansas senator is 8.8 years and of a representative, 5.8 years. Table 2.3 provides the data from which these averages were derived.[5]

Keeping tensions at a manageable level is a concern of administrators in most organizations. Legislative leaders are not exceptions in this respect, but they lead an organization in which factionalism, and therefore tension, is not only typical, it is institutionalized. Partisan conflict is considered to be functional. It is viewed in democratic ideology as necessary to accountability.

Keeping partisanship within limits can be a problem for legislative leaders, but it is usually less demanding than the task of achieving and maintaining cohesion within the legislative party that elected them to office. Among the explanations for centrifugal tendencies within legislative parties is the diversity of the constituencies and interests that legislators represent. One indicator of these differences is the occupations of Kansas legislators, the kinds of jobs on which

TABLE 2.4
THE OCCUPATIONS OF KANSAS LEGISLATORS, 1977

Occupations	Senate	House
Farmers/ranchers	8	30
Businessmen	5	18
Attorneys	12	16
Banking/finance	2	2
Real estate/insurance	3	12
Managers	1	6
Architects, engineers, contractors	1	6
Educators	1	5
Publishers	2	1
Laborers	0	5
Homemakers	1	4
Legislators	0	3
Students	0	3
Retired	0	4
Other	4	10

* As listed in the *Legislative Directory* for 1977–78.

they depend for their livelihoods. Table 2.4 depicts the variety of occupations from which citizen-legislators are recruited.

Whether differences in occupation, race, sex, religion, or age are significant factors in accounting for the absence of party cohesion on many issues is debatable. None of these variables has been shown to be a good predictor of legislative voting behavior.

From the perspective of organization theory the fact that most legislators are not dependent upon their legislative incomes to make ends meet is much more important than the differences referred to above. What the absence of dependence on the legislative job means is that the organization is relatively powerless to impose constraints upon the behavior of legislators. In that respect, a legislative organization is quite different from most other organizations in the public and private sectors.

ADMINISTRATORS

Forty senators and one hundred and twenty-five representatives are the masters in the Kansas legislature. Their requests are generally treated as commands by those employees who are not assigned to particular legislators. But most staff members, who work in six departments, take their orders from the administrators of those departments, who, in turn, consider themselves accountable to the seven-member Legislative Coordinating Council.

The word "department" is not the official designation for all of the six distinct staff operations, but it serves to mark out the boundaries of administrative authority. In the Legislative Research Department the director, the associate director, and the chief fiscal analyst hire and terminate employees and also allocate and supervise work assignments. The revisor of statutes and the first assistant revisor perform those same functions in the Office of the Revisor of Statutes. The post auditor, the deputy post auditor, and the assistant post auditor administer the Division of Legislative Post Audit. The director of legislative administrative services appoints and supervises most of the legislature's part-time employees, as well as a full-time staff.

The secretary of the Senate and the clerk of the House, who are accountable to the president of the Senate and the Speaker of the House, respectively, direct the desk operations in the Senate and the House, respectively.

Budgets, payrolls, schedules, records, personnel recruitment, production, and reports constitute the daily fare of legislative administrators. In the performance of those functions, the life of legislative administrators is hardly different from that of administrators generally. What complicates their jobs is the fact that they serve several masters who are not always in agreement as to what should be done. One administrator expressed his dilemma as follows: "I am given orders by one of the legislative leaders, and I worry about whether the other leaders want me to do what he tells me to do."

The job of a legislative administrator is further complicated by the necessity for him to be involved in the work of all of the principal staff persons he supervises. In protecting his suborganization from criticism that he would like to avoid, he has no alternative but to try to be informed about the activities of all staff members. Since some of the staff members work closely with committee chairmen, there is always the possibility that these members will come to behave as autonomous entrepreneurs in domains that they regard as their own. There is no practical way by which a legislative administrator can monopolize access to the masters, even if he is disposed to try. He must accommodate to a pluralistic environment in which a subordinate may develop independent access. Running a tight ship is an objective that most legislative administrators must forego.

But in the Kansas legislature, administrators enjoy relatively high job security. They can be dismissed only by concurrence of five of the seven members of the leadership group, the Coordinating Council. Moreover, they receive a very important tangible compensation in the form of involvement in many of the most important policy decisions that the legislature makes. They are where the action is, and for people who like the world of politics, that reward is as important as the salaries they earn.

PROFESSIONALS

The professionals are distinguishable from other legislative employees by the fact that the positions they hold require graduate degrees. All members of the staff of the revisor of statutes, save clerical employees and computer technicians, are lawyers. All members of the staffs of the Research Department and Post Audit, again except for clerical employees, have earned graduate degrees in any one of several fields. Most of them have obtained their graduate degrees in political science, public administration, or business administration. From graduate education the professionals presumably have acquired research skills, analytical capabilities, the ability to write coherently, and a general education that will be helpful to the policy-development roles they perform.

The professionals are not the only legislative employees whose services are vital in the maintenance of the lawmaking and overseeing technologies, but they form the staff upon whom the legislators depend for gathering and analyzing information. The professionals perform essentially the same judgmental-analytical tasks as legislators. But their votes are not counted when decisions are made, except in the sense that they may influence numbers of legislators.

Influence is a sensitive subject for professionals in the Kansas legislature. Most of them embrace the principle of neutral competence and prefer to believe that they can serve any legislative master. In practice, neutral competence is a difficult standard to maintain. In representing the intelligence that they assemble and express, it is hard not to be an advocate. A part of the professional's problem, in this respect, is the legislator who asks individual professionals to make known their judgments on policy issues. The more competent a professional is perceived to be, the more demanding are the pressures that the legislators exert on the staff in order to help them decide how to vote.

Though professionals enjoy a relatively high status in legislative organizations, their ability to be effective varies with the abilities of legislators to use staff services. Citizen-legislators, including committee chairpersons, are often unschooled in the potential advantages of staff expertise. By the same token, professionals are often unable to educate legislators to greater expectations of staff services, in part because professionals are apprehensive about being accused of preempting the legislator's decision-making role.

What seems evident in a legislative organization in which the legislators are part-time lawmakers is that the bills enacted would contain more deficiencies than they do if the services of professionals were not to be available tomorrow.

SECRETARIES AND CLERKS

It is a cliché that in many organizations the secretaries and clerks do the work for which their bosses receive the credit. There is enough truth in this saying to keep it alive. That the services of secretaries and clerks are considered indispensable in the Kansas legislature is evidenced by the fact that there are more of them than there are employees in any other category. They type letters, keep minutes, record decisions, transmit messages, read documents, and file the multitude of papers that every legislator and staff department receives. They are the indispensable links in the intricate network of communications that characterizes a legislative organization.

Because in the Kansas legislature most secretaries and clerks are part-time employees, they are not as helpful as their counterparts in Congress in socializing legislators to the means of performing legislative roles. Many secretaries and clerks are as much amateurs as the masters they serve. That fact must be regarded as a weakness in the operation of legislative technologies, but one that may be remedied in time.

Virtually all secretaries and most clerks in the Kansas legislature are women. Though more women are winning legislative seats and receiving administrative assignments than in the past, the Kansas legislature in 1977 remains an organization dominated by males.

RETAINERS

Doormen and sergeants at arms are the patronage employees of the Kansas legislature. They are generally retired men who are hired for jobs that require no special skills. Patience and a knowledge of who is authorized to enter the Senate and House chambers are the primary demands the organization makes on the individuals who perform roles in the retainer category.

Patronage is a somewhat misleading characterization of the process by which doormen and sergeants are recruited in the modern era, insomuch as it implies a turnover when control shifts from one party to another. The Democrats became the majority party in the House as a result of the general election of 1976, but none of the retainers who had previously been appointed by Republican leaders lost their jobs. But the expectation remains that vacancies will be filled by the Democratic leaders in the House and that people identified with the Democrats will be appointed if the Democrats retain control of the House.

The House sergeant at arms performs the ritualistic function of announcing the presence of the governor when he comes to address a joint session. Both the Senate and the House sergeants also find and bring to the floor the individual legislators who are absent when a call of the house is ordered.

Measured by responsibility, the status structure of the Kansas legislature is roughly equivalent to the order in which the five categories of employees are discussed in this chapter. The legislators alone are accountable to the citizens of Kansas for what the organization produces and fails to produce. The retainers are least responsible for the legislature's operations.

But that status structure does not conform to the salaries and wages that legislative employees receive. The administrators and professionals are the highest-paid employees. Several administrators earn more than three times the income that legislators derive from their positions. In 1977 a Kansas legislator received $35 per calendar day during the session and an additional $44 subsistence per calendar day. During the interim, each legislator received $200 per month for nine months, plus per diem and subsistence for those days when he attended committee meetings. If subsistence is included in calculating a legislator's income, each legislator earned about $10,000 in 1977.

Chart 2.1 identifies the staff units of the Kansas legislature and the formal lines of authority. Every person who receives a paycheck from the legislature works within one of the boxes on the chart. In a Spartan manner, the chart depicts what has been described in the preceding paragraphs, the specialization of tasks performed within the legislative organization. What are omitted that are relevant to specialization are the committee structure (the topic of the next chapter) and the special contributions of individuals who are participants in the activities of the legislature but are not on the legislature's payroll. This collectivity constitutes what organization theorists call the "task environment."

THE TASK ENVIRONMENT

The idea of a task environment is that any complex modern organization is dependent in one way or another on individuals and groups who are not members of that organization.[6] What this assumption implies is that a strategy for improving the efficiency of an organization's operations or a strategy for enhancing the effectiveness of an organization's outputs must take into account these dependencies. In the private sector, organizations endeavor to limit and control the task environment in order to ensure the stability and quality of their technologies. The motivation is clear: for example, a manufacturing enterprise is in trouble if needed raw materials are suddenly not available or if the supply is irregular and unpredictable.

Given the phenomenon of organizational dependence on components of the task environment, one may appropriately ask: Who are the participants in a legislative organization's activities whose names do not appear on the payroll? What is the nature of their involvement? What functions do they perform? Are the functions indispensable? Can a legislature effectively buffer its technologies from the influence of such groups? Should it endeavor to do so?

Some of these empirical and normative questions are addressed in chapters 4 and 5. In the remainder of this chapter we will identify the principal groups in the task environment upon which the Kansas legislature is dependent, and we will say something about the services that these groups provide and the problems that they create.

CHART 2.1

ORGANIZATION OF LEGISLATIVE STAFF AGENCIES IN KANSAS

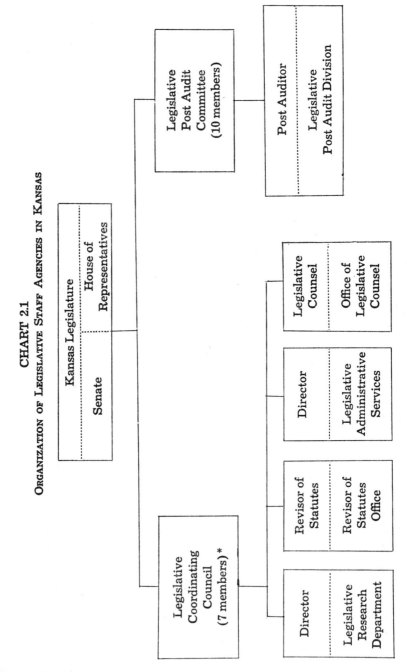

* Includes president of the Senate, the Speaker of the House, the Speaker pro tem, and the majority and minority leaders of the Senate and the House.

Personnel of the Executive Branch

In the office of the governor of Kansas two persons are designated as legislative liaison officers. Their task is to keep the governor informed as to the status of all bills in which the governor is interested, to expedite passage of the governor's bills, and to advise legislators about the probability that the governor will sign or veto certain bills if they come to his desk.

It is customary for governors to appoint former legislators to the liaison positions, though in 1977 only one of those positions was occupied by a former legislator. The other position was held by a former executive secretary of the Kansas Board of Regents. A firsthand knowledge of the lawmaking process is considered to be a necessary qualification. A secondary qualification is acquaintance with legislators, particularly those who hold leadership positions.

Though the governor is not a legislative employee, he is a constitutional participant in the lawmaking process. By his state of the state message, his budget message, and special messages he contributes to the legislature's agenda. By his vote on all bills that pass both houses in identical form, he shares with legislators the task of making decisions.

The governor is the only officer in the executive branch who is a constitutional participant in the lawmaking process. His subordinates, secretaries of departments, heads of agencies, and other agency personnel participate in the deliberations on bills that affect the operations of their agencies. They may exercise initiative in trying to influence legislative decision-making, or they may be called to testify before one or more committees of the Senate and the House.

In Kansas there are few uniformities with respect to agency involvement in the legislative arena. In some departments the secretary alone interacts with legislators and legislative committees. In others, that responsibility is delegated to various officers, depending on the nature of the bill being considered. Some agencies are aggressive participants in legislative decision-making; others rarely become directly involved in influencing legislative actions.

There are more than two hundred agencies of the executive branch in the government of Kansas. The fact that so few of them maintain an active liaison with the legislature is at least partly attributable to the standard that agency personnel should not engage in lobbying.

Representatives of Interest Groups

In Kansas, lobbyists are required to register in the Office of the Secretary of State and to report receipts and expenditures. During the 1977 session, 361 persons registered. Table 2.5 lists the number of lobbyists on the list of registrants by type of organization represented.

Lobbyists are selective participants. Generally, they ignore all bills that do not appear to have an impact on the interests of the organizations they represent. But in order to identify bills that are potentially effective, they are obliged to review all bills introduced and to study some of them carefully. The association of major oil companies is one of the interest groups that assist their lobbyists by staff analyses of bills in the regional headquarters of the organization.

Any number of bills are introduced in each session at the behest of interest groups, so it is appropriate to note that lobbyists not only react to bills that legislators introduce; they also play a role in agenda-building (a function discussed in chapter 5).

In *The Kansas Legislature* it was noted that one explanation for the influence of interest groups in lawmaking is that most legislators are unclear about the opinions of their constituencies on most issues and that the positions of interest groups provide legislators with a

TABLE 2.5

REGISTERED REPRESENTATIVES OF INTEREST GROUPS, BY TYPE AND NUMBER, 1977

Type of Organization Represented	Number of Lobbyists
Agriculture	18
Business*	46
Education	32
Finance	18
Government (city, county)	25
Industry*	47
Insurance	40
Labor	26
Professional	35
Religious	8
Social	34
Utilities	32
Total	**361**

* The business category includes small industries and business associations, whereas the industry category includes the larger corporations.

reading on how segments of their constituencies will react to certain bills if they are enacted.[7] In this respect the legislative organization is dependent upon interest groups. The intelligence that lobbyists provide is more than specialized kinds of information; for they are barometers of intensity of feeling and belief.

THE MEDIA

During the 1977 session of the Kansas legislature, twenty reporters covered the state capitol. Seven represented the wire services. Five covered for television and radio stations. The other eight were correspondents from the Harris News Service, the *Topeka Daily Capital* and *Journal*, the *Wichita Eagle* and *Beacon*, and the *Kansas City Star* and *Times*.

It is assumed that legislators need reporters in order to keep their constituents informed and that reporters need the legislators in action in order to have something to report. But if legislators and reporters are functionally interdependent, this isn't always evident. Individuals in one group often talk as though the other group were expendable. The adversary relationship doesn't quite fit the idea of a task environment—that is, that the operation of legislative technologies is in some way dependent upon the media. And yet, the absence of news coverage would increase the uncertainties that attend policy-making. Anticipating public response to certain kinds of decisions is difficult under the best of conditions, so it is reasonable to argue that correspondents assist the legislature by the citizen feedback that they generate. They also serve as conduits of information within the legislative organization by telling legislators and staff what other legislators and staff are doing. The newspapers and the television and radio news programs are a part of the legislature's communication system.

Until an open-meetings law was enacted, the legislature was able to buffer press influence on decision-making in committees and in caucuses: executive sessions were the buffering devices. Today it is difficult to justify closed meetings, so they rarely occur. Communication among legislators and between staff and legislators can be kept confidential only through informal meetings of small groups inside and outside the Statehouse.

Except for most legislative staff members and selected agents of the executive branch, only reporters are given free access to the floor of the House and the Senate when sessions are in progress. In that respect, media representatives are privileged over other groups of nonorganization members who are participants in the legislative arena.

PERSONNEL OF THE JUDICIAL BRANCH

In 1977 the state of Kansas had 69 judges of district courts, 7 judges of appellate courts, and 7 members of the Supreme Court. If to this number of judicial officers are added the state's attorney general and his legal staff,[8] approximately 18 lawyers, the legal component of the legislature's task environment numbers 101 persons.

Only the attorney general and his staff interact with legislators frequently. Interactions occur because any legislator may ask the attorney general for a statutory or constitutional interpretation. During the 1977 session, approximately fifty such requests were initiated by legislators or legislative staff acting in behalf of legislators.

Because the attorney general challenges the legality of legislative decisions on occasion, the legislature in 1974 created the office of legislative counsel. It is the function of the counsel to provide legislators with legal advice that is independent of the services of the attorney general and to represent the legislature in litigation in which legislators may be parties or in which the legislature has an interest. The creation of the office of counsel was an effort of the legislature to limit its dependence on the office of the attorney general.[9]

The recent case of the constitutionality of the State Finance Council (*State of Kansas, ex rel., Curt T. Schneider, Attorney General, v. Robert Bennett, Governor of the State of Kansas, et al., 1977*) illustrates the roles of the judges, the attorney general, and the legislative counsel. On constitutional grounds, the attorney general initiated action in the Shawnee County District Court to prevent the State Finance Council from executing certain statutory powers. The district court granted the petition.[10] Subsequently, the State Supreme Court reversed the decision and entered judgment for the defendants.[11] The legislative counsel filed briefs amicus curiae for the Kansas Senate, the Kansas House, and the Legislative Coordinating Council in both cases.

At issue were statutory powers that were alleged to be in violation of the principles of separation of powers and delegation of powers. The legislature had created an instrumentality for performing certain functions (see chapter 5). The attorney general challenged the instrument on legal grounds. The counsel represented the legislature's interests. The courts adjudicated the controversy.

From the perspective adopted in this treatise, all these parties, save the counsel, are parts of the legislature's task environment. They are relatively independent of legislative control, but they must be reckoned with because they can affect the legislature's ability to perform certain functions in certain ways. The legislature can seek to buffer the influence of the attorney general and the courts on legislative operations, but it cannot ignore their presence in the legislative arena. The decision to create an office of legislative counsel constituted overt recognition of the kind of task-environment dependency that has been illustrated in this section.

SUMMARY

The payroll of the Kansas legislature is the indicator of organization membership used in this analysis. By examining the types of job descriptions of those who work for the legislature and the grouping of these positions by function and for managerial purposes, the specialization of tasks and the authority structure—two conditions characteristic of all complex organizations—come into bold relief.

It is decidedly unusual for an organization to have 165 "masters," but with respect to its categories of employees (administrators, professionals, secretaries and clerks, and retainers) it is not atypical. The counterparts of these job types could be found in many private and public organizations.

In addition to the participants who are members of the legislative organization, there are participants who belong to other organizations. The latter constitute the task environment of the legislature, participants upon whom the legislature is dependent in a variety of ways. Generally characteristic of the relationship between the legislative organization and the task environment are the following: (1) The legislature selectively buffers its technologies from influences of the task environment. (2) Participants in the task environment are highly selective about where and when they choose to be involved in the legislative process.

3
The Committees

Most complex modern organizations assign tasks to groups as well as to individuals. Committees are formed to analyze problems and to generate or evaluate proposals for the solution of problems. The organizational goals of effective communication and coordination are often achieved through the committee device. And increasingly, policy decisions are being made by committees.

But generalizations about the role of committees in American organizational life are not likely to be very helpful to those who need or want to know about the committee systems of state legislatures. Those systems exhibit special characteristics which, taken together, make them unique. An analysis of the committee system of the Kansas legislature provides a case in point.

PART 1

There are four types of legislative committees which in Kansas are institutionalized: the committee of the whole, standing committees, interim committees, and conference committees.[1] The first, the second, and the fourth have existed from the 1860s; the third type, interim committees, has evolved during the past five decades.

The committee of the whole is a committee the membership of which, in the House, includes every representative and, in the Senate, every senator. Each chamber resolves itself into a committee of the whole for consideration of bills on the calendar of general orders. The symbolic aspect of a committee is maintained by the practice of designating a member other than the Speaker in the House, or the president in the Senate, to preside over these sessions and by the practice of deciding whether to *recommend* a bill for passage. The substantive characteristic is that it is in committee of the whole that bills are explained, debated, and amended. In the next chapter it will be argued that the principal function of the committee of the whole in the lawmaking technology is to project the possible consequences of enacting or failing to enact a bill.

The standing committees of the Kansas legislature (nineteen in the House and sixteen in the Senate) constitute the second and best-known feature of the legislative organization. They review most of the bills that are introduced during a session or are carried over from the previous session. Essentially, standing committees decide whether a bill merits consideration by the committee of the whole. In effect, standing committees *screen* bills. Their decisions are made known by motions to report a bill favorably or unfavorably, or, in some cases, by failure to take any action.

Table 3.1 identifies the subject-matter responsibilities of standing committees (by title) and the number of members of each committee. The fact that Senate committees generally include fewer members than House committees is evident from the table. The significance of that difference will be discussed later in this chapter.

Because standing committees conduct hearings on certain bills, one should note that the committees formally interact with individuals and groups of the task environment. Only during hearings do interest groups and agency administrators, primary components of the task environment, perform a semiofficial role in the lawmaking process. They enjoy access to individual legislators prior to, during, and after sessions; but that access depends upon factors other than legislative structure or procedure.

The third type of committee in the Kansas legislature is the interim committee. Meeting between sessions, interim committees study problems that have been assigned to them by resolution of the House or the Senate and, more frequently, by the seven-member leadership group, the Coordinating Council. Interim committees prepare reports,

TABLE 3.1

STANDING COMMITTEES OF THE KANSAS LEGISLATURE

Title of Committee	Number of Members
House	
Agriculture and Livestock	21
Assessment and Taxation	21
Calendar and Printing	7
Claims and Accounts	7
Commercial and Financial Institutions	19
Energy and Natural Resources	21
Education	21
Elections	17
Federal and State Affairs	21
Governmental Organization	15
Insurance	15
Interstate Cooperation	7
Judiciary	19
Labor and Industry	17
Legislative, Judicial, and Congressional Apportionment	15
Local Government	21
Public Health and Welfare	19
Rules and Journal	5
Transportation	21
Ways and Means	23
Senate	
Agriculture and Livestock	11
Assessment and Taxation	11
Commercial and Financial Institutions	11
Education	11
Elections	9
Energy and Natural Resources	11
Federal and State Affairs	11
Governmental Organization	9
Judiciary	13
Labor and Industry	9
Legislative, Congressional, and Judicial Apportionment	11
Local Government	11
Organization, Calendar, and Rules	7
Public Health and Welfare	11
Transportation and Utilities	11
Ways and Means	11
Joint Committee of the House and Senate	
Special Claims	5

and they prepare bills if the majority of the members of a committee believe it appropriate to do so.

Generally, interim committees are composed of both senators and representatives. Legislators are assigned to interim committees by the Legislative Coordinating Council. Table 3.2 lists the problems that were assigned to interim committees in 1977. In the next chapter the role of interim committees in the first stage of the lawmaking process —namely, agenda-building—will be considered.

The fourth type of committee in the Kansas legislature is the conference committee. Composed of both senators and representatives, conference committees seek to reconcile differences between House and Senate versions of a bill. Thir activities constitute the sixth stage of the lawmaking technology, a bargaining or negotiating process.

The four types of committees briefly described above are relatively permanent features of the Kansas legislative organization today. Each type performs functions that are considered necessary to the technology of lawmaking. The number of legislators, the volume of bills, the uncertainties that attend reliance on elements of the task environment for agenda items, the limitations of time, constitutional requirements, and the bicameral structure of the legislature—all help to explain the present committee structure.

Unlike members of many ad hoc and ongoing committees in corporate organizations, who are specialists of one kind or another, members of legislative committees are generalists. Individuals may request to serve on standing committees or interim committees that consider matters related to their nongovernmental occupations (e.g., farmers asking to serve on the Committee on Agriculture), but their appointment to such committees does not really change the generalist character of legislative committees. Legislators become specialists when, over time, they become knowledgeable about the delivery of governmental services in the functional area of committee responsibility and about the nature of the problems that are more or less persistent in that area. Given the high turnover of legislators in the citizen legislature of Kansas, few legislators become specialists.

Specialization would be an inevitable development in Kansas legislative committees if the seniority system were institutionalized and if being a legislator were to become a full-time occupation. But in 1977 neither development appears likely. The leaders show no

TABLE 3.2

PROBLEMS ASSIGNED TO INTERIM COMMITTEES OF THE KANSAS LEGISLATURE,
1977–78 SESSION

Committee	Problems
Agriculture and Livestock	Seed Laboratory and seed laws Filled milk and filled-milk products
Assessment and Taxation	Taxation of personal property Inheritance tax Sales tax Income tax State aid to local units Solar-energy tax incentives
Commercial and Financial Institutions	Privacy of financial records Usury rate for savings and loan associations Equal credit opportunity Group health insurance contracts
Corrections	Correctional programs and facilities
Elections	Governmental Ethics Commission Campaign Finance Act Presidential preference primary Voter registration
Energy	Energy conservation Rate-making principles and rate structures Energy research and production Construction work in progress Municipal utility rates and state jurisdiction Wheeling of electrical power
Federal and State Affairs	Annual state census Insulation standards Physically handicapped standards State real estate transactions
Judicial Compensation	Judicial compensation
Judiciary—A	Product liability Delegation of legislative authority Mental illness statutes

TABLE 3.2 (continued)

PROBLEMS ASSIGNED TO INTERIM COMMITTEES OF THE KANSAS LEGISLATURE,
1977–78 SESSION

Committee	Problems
	Department of Justice
	Court costs
	Uniform Exemptions Act
	Uniform Land Transfers and Land Sales Practices Acts
	Initiative and referendum
Judiciary—B	Juvenile Code
	Lien laws
	Expungement of criminal records—annulment of convictions
	Determinate sentencing
	Death with dignity
	Sale of franchises
	"Child grabbing" (or child custody)
	Requirements governing criminal history records
Kansas-Missouri Boundary	True Kansas-Missouri boundary establishment
Labor and Industry	Review of Workmen's Compensation Law
	Review of Employment Security Law
Legislative Budget	State General Fund
	Fiscal notes
	State personnel system
	Capitol area plaza
	Contracting for computer services
	State warrants reconciliation
	Tort Claims Act
Legislative Educational Planning (1202 Commission)	Postsecondary educational planning
Local Government	Review of Municipal Bond Laws
	Park and recreation programs
	Cemetery perpetual care funds
Natural Resources	Water-related issues
	Well-inspection personnel

TABLE 3.2 (concluded)
PROBLEMS ASSIGNED TO INTERIM COMMITTEES OF THE KANSAS LEGISLATURE,
1977–78 SESSION

Committee	*Problems*
Public Health and Welfare	Credentials for health-care personnel Physician extenders
School Finance	School finance
Transportation and Utilities	City connecting links Vehicle registration fee schedules International truck registration plan Declining highway revenues
Use Value Assessment	Use value assessment

Ways and Means—A	Community mental-health and
	   retardation facilities
	State SRS institutions and programs
	Wichita branch, University of Kansas
	   Medical Center
	Kansas utilization of Title XX
	Retention of medical school graduates
	   in Kansas
	Energy utilization and sources
	Rainbow Unit review
	Computerization of health-related fee
	   agencies licensure data

Ways and Means—B	Personnel of district courts
	Court unification costs and financing
	Zero-based budgeting and Sunset
	   Laws
	Financing of vocational education
	State building construction procedures
	Review of the Department of
	   Transportation
	Review of the Forestry, Fish and
	   Game Commission policies for
	   farming contracts
	K.B.I. facility

disposition to give up their prerogative of naming committee chairmen and members, and there is considerable resistance to extending the time of legislative sessions and to increasing salaries to a level that would permit legislators to treat their positions as full-time occupations.

Standing and interim committees in the Kansas legislature are staffed by professionals who develop expertise in policy areas. That fact tends to offset the lack of specialization by committee members. Each standing committee is served by two professionals of the Legislative Research Department (one of whom is the principal) and one professional from the Office of the Revisor of Statutes. Though these professionals are not hired to staff particular committees, they are generally kept on as staff members for particular committees, a tendency that encourages subject-matter expertise.

But in a sense, professional staff members are always generalists, even though they become knowledgeable about specific governmental activities and problems. The changing character of the environment in which legislatures function confronts staff with situations in which their previous experience has only a limited applicability. Moreover, uncertainty attends the consequences of most policy decisions, a condition that is not apt to change until and unless analysis of policy becomes more sophisticated than it is at present.

The duplication of standing committees, one set in the House and one in the Senate—a consequence of bicameralism—is a characteristic of legislative committee systems that is not usually found in the systems of other complex organizations. The advantages of committee duplication in a legislative organization are not likely to be perceived as advantages in other organizations. The duplication of policy committees in a corporation would be viewed as unnecessarily costly in time and energy. But the uncertainties that accompany many policy proposals argue in favor of duplicate review of those proposals. An additional justification stems from the belief that political influences may cause a committee to act favorably or unfavorably on a bill without regard to its merit (that is, without thought to long-range consequences).

Some state legislatures have moved to eliminate duplication by creating joint standing committees. To date, this suggested change has not been adopted by the Kansas legislature. Interim committees, however, are usually joint committees. It is assumed that the advantages of duplicating of committees do not apply when the purposes are to study problems and to develop proposals rather than to screen or evaluate proposals submitted in bill form.

In many organizations, committees are essentially advisory rather than decision-making. In legislatures, including the Kansas legislature, established procedures make it difficult to override a committee's judgment in lawmaking as well as in overseeing the operations of the executive branch. Though many committee decisions must be ratified by actions of House and Senate members, each chamber's practical choice is to agree or disagree rather than to amend the substance of the decision. This is particularly true in respect to conference-committee reports, which, according to the rules of the House and Senate, cannot be amended on the floor.

Coordination of work activities is a committee task in many private and public organizations, but in the Kansas legislature, coordination is accomplished primarily by legislative leaders and administrators. It is the primary internal or organizational role of the president of the Senate, the Speaker of the House, and the majority and minority floor leaders in both houses. Though armed with authority to make certain kinds of coordinative decisions by issuing directives or orders, these leaders generally employ persuasion. This practice makes understandable the political scientist's contention that legislative leaders are primarily engaged in consensus-building. But it is appropriate to note that legislative technologies will break down unless time and energy are given to making the system work irrespective of the manner in which the coordinative tasks are performed. That judgment will be extended and illustrated in chapter 6, "The Role of Leadership."

PART 2

The types of committees, the generalist backgrounds of committee participants, the staffing, the duplication of standing committees, the decision-making powers of committees, and the nonuse of committees for coordination are differentiating characteristics of a legislative committee system, particularly the committee system of the Kansas legislature. Though the system is formalized, continuing, and stable, it is not free from problems. During recent years, organizational assessments have recognized a number of difficulties.

1. Because the effectiveness of committees is dependent upon the skills of the chairmen and because the capabilities of chairmen vary from able to inept, committee performance in the Kansas legislature is far from uniform. This judgment, though it is widely shared by organizational participants, participants in the task environment, and observers, has not inspired any organized efforts to remedy the weakness. Speakers of the House have removed committee chairmen who were "guilty" of being tedious or who were unable to move their committees to report out bills expeditiously; but in part because the leaders are elective and so depend upon support from the party caucus, they are unwilling to exercise that authority except when protests increase.

Turnover is yet another reason for the persistence of the problem of inept committee chairmen. Legislators learn how to chair a meeting by practice over a period of time. If they haven't developed the skills of presiding before they become legislators, they may not serve as committee chairmen long enough to learn how to plan a meeting, how to keep discussion germane, how to control compulsive talkers, how to utilize staff services effectively, and how to make procedural rules serve the seemingly contradictory purposes of expediting action while maintaining the principles of majority rule and minority rights.

The problem of turnover is not easily solved. Of the reasons for turnover of committee chairmen indicated in table 3.3, only one, the movement of chairmen from one committee to another, is subject to the control of legislative leaders. They might, for example, combine certain minor committees, thus evening out the work load of committees and thereby reducing the incentive of legislators to move from minor to major committee chairmanships.

It is true, of course, that expertise in subject matter is a function of committee membership rather than committee leadership. One may be knowledgeable about a category of policy problems without having had the experience of serving as a committee chairman. But once again, turnover is a problem. If we total the number of years of committee services of senators on three major committees in 1977, we

TABLE 3.3

NUMBER OF AND REASONS FOR TURNOVER OF CHAIRMEN OF STANDING
COMMITTEES, BY CHAMBER, 1961–77

	Senate	House	Total
Defeated for reelection	13	11	24
Elected to position of legislative leadership	3	2	5
Moved to chair another committee	5	5	10
Became candidate for or was appointed to a nonlegislative office	3	5	8
Retired or resigned from office	7	21	28
Change in party control	0	15*	15

* Fifteen Republican committee chairmen were reelected to the House in 1976, but were then replaced as chairmen by the Democratic Speaker.

discover that 5.3 years is the average length of service on the Ways and Means Committee; 2.5 years, on the Judiciary Committee; and 3.5 years, on the Education Committee. In the House the average length of service on the Ways and Means Committee is 3.6 years; on the Judiciary Committee, 2.8 years; and on the Education Committee, 1.9 years.

2. The number of committee members appears to impede effective dialogue. If eight to twelve members is considered ideal, every Senate standing committee save one is of appropriate size, but only four of the House committees meet that standard (see table 3.1). A veteran professional compared the House and the Senate committees on Assessment and Taxation and concluded that the latter proceeded by discussion to explore most aspects of a problem. In contrast, the deliberations of the House committee were rarely thorough and comprehensive, a difference that he attributed to size as well as to personalities.

Unless the House is willing to enlarge the number of standing committees to accommodate the interests of 125 legislators, a remedy that introduces problems that originally caused a reduction in the numbers of committees, the creation of subcommittees appears to be the only feasible means of enhancing the opportunities for discussion. Another option that is advocated occasionally is to interrupt legislative sessions for periods of time during which only committee meetings would occur.

3. Effective use of professional staff is yet another problem of the

committee system in the Kansas legislature. Many legislators, including chairmen of committees, do not know what to expect of staff services. Sometimes staff expertise is not utilized as committees deliberate in ignorance of available information. Often hearings are conducted, and those appearing are not questioned intensively or carefully, an omission that might be remedied in part by assistance from the staff.

Though the committee system is primary in the group structure of the Kansas legislature, mention should be made of the party caucus and informal groups. They are kinds of groups that are formed in all state legislative organizations. Both perform a cue-providing function; that is, they help legislators to identify shared interests that are reflected in voting patterns. Though these kinds of groups are important to political scientists who focus on the politics of a legislature, they are outside the purview of this study, an analysis of the Kansas legislature as an organization.

Having identified the participants by categories of tasks performed and having outlined the organized group structure, the committee system, we turn to the dominant and subdominant technologies of the Kansas legislature.

4
Lawmaking:
The Dominant Technology

Not all that is "process" is technology.[1] In the theory of organizational behavior, in which technology has become one of the central concepts, technology means that part of the process that is formally structured and generally perceived as instrumental to the attainment of the purposes for which the organization exists. Put another way, technology is deliberate procedure, procedure that, given the goals and characteristics of an organization, is adopted as a rational means of converting inputs into outputs.

There are, of course, several ways of accomplishing most purposes of an organization. Alternative means are alternative technologies. But the choices are usually limited by the characteristics of the organization. In this sense, characteristics are constraints. Some proposed modifications of an organization's technology are rejected precisely because they are viewed as inconsistent with one or more characteristics that the leaders and members of an organization cannot or will not relinquish. For example, a decision to eliminate public hearings by legislative committees might expedite decision-making, but the cost of that change would be some diminution of the legislature's responsive or representative characteristic, a trade-off that legislators are not likely to accept.

Though technology is a more specific focus than process, it is broad enough to encompass the thought that all organizations operate one or more technologies. The procedures by which the Rand Corporation develops strategies for coping with a problem are no less technologies than the organized manner in which General Motors produces an automobile. An ordered procedure for the conversion of ideas fits the concept of technology, as does the procedure by which physical resources are converted into physical objects. The conversion procedure of a legislature is lawmaking. Lawmaking is the legislature's dominant technology.

In part 1 of this chapter the sequential, seven-phase, lawmaking procedure of the Kansas legislature is described and analyzed. The analysis is based on the following assumptions: (1) At each stage a certain kind of analytical-judgmental activity occurs which is logical—that is, instrumental—to the lawmaking function.[2] (2) Though the legislature, like all complex organizations, is dependent on the environment, the involvement of components of the task environment varies from phase to phase.[3] (3) The legislature buffers dependence on environment differentially.[4] Table 4.1 provides an overview of the analytical scheme.

In part 2 of this chapter the characteristics of a legislature, which both help to explain the procedure and which limit the options that may be considered in changing the technology, are identified. Constitutional limitations (employing the word "constitutional" in its broadest sense) are externally imposed imperatives that put constraints on technological innovation.

PART 1

Phase 1: Agenda-building

A legislature does not manufacture the problems it chooses to consider (though some critics occasionally charge a legislature with doing just that), except that in every session some bills are introduced to correct or clean up laws previously enacted. Although most of the problems that a legislature considers may be said to originate in the environment, not all the problems that one or more citizens perceive become inputs into the legislative technology. Only when a legislator or committee of legislators decides that a problem is subject to legislative solution and then decides that it should be considered

TABLE 4.1

LAWMAKING, THE DOMINANT TECHNOLOGY: AN ANALYTICAL SCHEME

Phase	Activity*	Task Environment†	Buffers‡
1. Agenda–building	Considering	Multiple groups	Interim committees Committee appointments Interim study decisions
2. Bill-drafting	Transforming	The courts Executive agencies	Staff organization and procedure
3. Committee action	Screening (winnowing)	Interest groups Legislative parties	Committee rules
4. Debate on General Orders	Projecting	Multiple groups	House and Senate rules
5. Final action	Deciding	Multiple groups	House and Senate rules
6. Conference Committees	Bargaining	Multiple groups	No fixed place or time of meeting
7. Gubernatorial vetoes	Confronting	Political parties	House and Senate rules

* The "dominance" of activity by stage should not be construed to mean that that kind of activity does not occur at other stages.

† "Multiple groups" means that the interests of no particular component of the task environment are given primary consideration.

‡ Buffers are organizationally imposed limits on access. House and Senate rules include constitutional requirements as well as those that are subject to change by House and Senate resolutions.

does a problem become an item on the legislature's agenda. The exceptions to this generalization are the governor's orders for executive reorganization, requirements for reapportionment, and appropriation bills.

The decision to consider is a cognitive act that triggers the legislative technology. All the problems and/or proposals that legislators decide to consider constitute the legislative agenda for a session. Agenda-building is the first phase of the legislative process.

Agenda-building activities link the legislative technology to the environment, whether a problem proposal is formulated and articulated by a nonlegislator or by a legislator. Even when a legislator acts on his own perception (takes the initiative), that action is a product of environmental influences. In that sense, all agenda items originate in the environment.

But that observation does not explain why some problem proposals become a part of the institutional agenda, while others do not. Are the decisions to consider and not to consider predictable? What happens during that agenda-building phase of the legislative process?

In the scenario constructed by group theorists, legislative agendas result from demands of interest groups. Disturbances of one kind or another cause persons to act in order to protect a shared interest, and inevitably they gravitate into political arenas, where, as David Easton put it, values are allocated authoritatively.[5] Since legislators are members of organized or potential interest groups, it doesn't make any difference where the initiative occurs. The implication of their analysis is that items on the legislative agenda are predictable from a knowledge of disturbances that are of sufficient intensity to cause interaction, providing that those who are disturbed enjoy or are able to obtain access. "Access" may be defined as the inclination of a legislator to consider the demands of an interest group, a disposition that is dependent upon the legislator's perception of his own interests.[6]

According to another interpretation, that of elite theory, legislators as a whole are portrayed as establishmentarians who screen out problems and proposals that are outside the parameters of elitist interests. Only when members of the establishment request inclusion of items on the agenda or when the items are regarded as consistent with elitist ideology are those items likely to be considered.[7]

From still another perspective, the theory of democracy, legislators are likely to consider a problem if a number of their voting constituents want it to be considered. Because legislators are accountable to their constituents in periodic elections, they are likely to place a problem on the agenda unless there is a compelling reason for not doing so.[8]

All these theories are suggestive of the conditions that affect the decisions of legislators to consider, decisions that trigger the legislative technology.

What can be learned from the psychology of decision-making that is relevant to understanding the agenda-building process? Though they perceive human behavior as responses to stimuli, scholars observe that a response cannot be predicted merely by knowing the nature of the stimulus. The attitudes, beliefs, and values of the respondent are at least as important in explanation as the stimulus. "What a person wants and likes influences what he sees; what he sees influences what he wants and likes."[9] There is a complex weaving of affective and cognitive processes.

Dimension is added by the observations that "an individual can attend to only a limited number of things at a time,"[10] that an individual's definitions of a situation will be different from the objective situation because handling complexity is difficult, and that individuals tend to evaluate proposals for action only in terms of subgoals. The last of these findings is highly relevant to agenda-building. What it means is that legislators tend to perceive goals as operational and nonoperational. Generally speaking, in order to be considered for inclusion on the legislative agenda, a problem proposal must be viewed as operational, that is, addressable by legislation.

However helpful these insights may be in understanding why some problems and/or proposals are put on the agenda, while others are not, the fact remains that the agenda-building phase of legislative technology is difficult to pattern.

When we turn to the question of what components of the task environment are most influential in the agenda-building process, we move on to more certain terrain. The governor, the executive-branch agencies, the federal and local governments, the media, and organized interest groups constitute the principal contributors to legislative agenda. What the governor decides should be considered is usually included on the agenda by virtue of the governor's constitutional duty to provide the legislature with a program and because the governor is a participant in the legislative process. He votes on every measure that passes both houses, and his vote counts for more than one.

Agencies of the executive branch enjoy a similar, though less certain, access to legislative agenda-building. Their responsibility for implementation of laws creates the presumption on the part of legislators that what the agencies want considered should be considered. That advantage may be lost, however, if an agency head becomes a *persona non grata* to the legislators who oversee that agency's operations.

Generally, it is through agency communications or the monitoring activities of analysts in the Legislative Research Department that the federal government influences legislative agendas. When Congress enacts a program involving a categorical grant or a bloc grant, or when it enacts any other kind of measure that calls for state action or that impinges on state government in any way, either a state agency of the executive branch or the Research Department is the first to know about it. Both interpret and advise legislators about federal actions, serving thereby as conduits through which the federal government feeds proposals into the legislative technology.

Local governments, another component of the task environment, are generally less dependent upon state agencies for access to the agenda-building process. It is usually sufficient for the spokesmen of these governments to contact the legislators who represent the district in which these governments are located. Additional access is provided by standing or special committees that have been created to review the needs of local governments.

That organized interest groups participate in agenda-building is symbolized by the fact that many of them develop a legislative program prior to a session, and some of them do so in an institutionalized manner. Having achieved access to one or more legislators, established interest groups are virtually assured that at least some part of their programs will be considered. The perceived ability of certain interest groups to affect the elections of certain legislators is a potent and continuing leverage in the construction of agendas. By the same token, those organized interest groups whose programs are considered to be politically dangerous by most legislators experience considerable difficulty in influencing agenda-building.

Thus far, the analysis of phase 1 of a legislature's dominant technology suggests almost complete dependence of a legislature on task-environment elements in agenda-building. By what activities does a legislative organization buffer that dependence? The answer is that buffering occurs directly through studies of problems conducted by interim committees and indirectly through the formal and informal processes of communications and socialization. When the leaders appoint interim committees and assign study projects to them, the legislature as an organization undertakes to provide some of its own inputs and to develop its own legislative program or agenda. To be sure, interim committees may call task-environment groups to testify, but they are expected to develop their own recommendations and, if appropriate, bills to implement them.

Buffering also occurs in indirect and more subtle ways. The legislative organization affects the selective attention of members through formal and informal communications by assignment to committees. Since the "vast bulk of our knowledge of fact is not gained through direct perception but through the second-hand, third-hand, and nth-hand reports of the perceptions of others,"[11] the legislature's channels of social communication inevitably affect the decisions to consider problems and/or proposals.

The legislature also affects the perceptual filters of members by formal and informal processes of socialization. When internalized, the goals and objectives of the organization may enlarge or narrow the perceptual lenses.

Finally, through interactions with knowledgeable staff and according to the way that certain kinds of bills are treated by leaders and members, the decisions to consider are encouraged or discouraged.

It should be apparent that the decisions to consider, which constitute the essential activity in agenda-building, do not imply intent to deal with a problem and/or proposal in depth, nor do they warrant any inference about the subsequent treatment of the proposals. Often, but not inevitably, the only follow-up action that will occur is that a bill will be drafted; that is, the proposals will proceed through the next phase of the dominant technology.

Because decisions of priority tend to be decisions of the leaders of legislative organizations, with or without the advice of the members, that activity will be analyzed in chapter 7, which is concerned with the role of leadership.

Given the relatively unstructured and unpredictable nature of legislative agenda-building, it is questionable whether this phase of activity should be treated as a part of the legislative technology. Not many uniformities are observable. Although labeling this varied activity as "considering" may overstate its cognitive aspects, it is the beginning of organizational activity. It is the "input" stage, without which there would be no legislative process, no legislative technology.

In this sense, agenda-building (considering) is functionally necessary. To be sure, agenda-building can and does occur at any time before a legislative session is ended, but it is most characteristic of legislative activity before and during the early part of a session. Viewing the process as sequential, we find that agenda-building is the first phase of the dominant technology.

Phase 2: Bill-Drafting

No fact lends more credence to the concept of technology than that most proposals involving the resolution or management of problems must be transformed into bills before they can be further considered after decisions about agenda-building have been made. Bill-drafting is a highly technical, professional skill—a technology that is generally understood as being peculiar to legislative organizations but is not generally appreciated for its significance. To the outsider, the requirement that proposals be put in bill form may appear to be as trivial as, for example, requiring that communications be typed on 8½ by 11 inch white paper. But trivial it is not.

Bill-drafting involves one or both of two kinds of analytical activities: (1) finding a solution to a problem, and (2) anticipating the most basic questions that must be answered before an enactment can be implemented. Though both of these analytical activities have been routinized, the processes are hardly mechanical. The judgmental aspects of constructing a bill are key variables in predicting the impact of a legislative output, or a law. A poorly drafted bill can effectively prevent reaching the objectives or goals that the problem proposal is intended to achieve.

The first of the analytical activities—finding a solution to a problem—occurs when a legislator asks a bill-drafter to design a bill to meet a problem but offers little or no guidance beyond a statement of the problem. For example, a legislator asks a bill-drafter to prepare a bill that will protect home owners from mechanics' liens resulting from the failure of a building contractor to pay his construction bills. The legislator assumes that the bill-drafter can discover ways of accomplishing this end through legal research. The bill-drafter then begins a searching process (sometimes with the assistance of the Research Department), which is familiar because of repetition. He seeks to know whether the problem has surfaced before, and if so, where, how the problem was handled, how basic and tangential issues were decided by the courts, and whether the law is changing (and if so, the direction of change). *American Jurisprudence, Corpus Juris Secundum*, court reports, *Law Weekly*, laws of the states, and law journals are the bill-drafter's principal tools. In our hypothetical case, the bill-drafter discovered that the state of New Jersey had enacted a comprehensive law to protect the rights of home owners, and that law afforded a model that the bill-drafter could use.

The second kind of analytical activity—anticipating "basic" questions—occupies most of the bill-drafter's time. Two components of the task environment constitute the principal points of reference: those who will administer the proposed law and the courts that will resolve any legal questions arising out of controversies over provisions of the proposed law.

For those who will administer the law, it is essential that the mandate or prohibition of the proposed law be clearly stated; that the means of implementation, whether one or several, be unambiguously specified; that the source of funds for implementation (if money is required) be specified (if not specified, then included in the omnibus appropriations bill); and that any rights of parties that may be affected be identified and safeguarded. In order to preclude ambiguities that will allow differences of interpretation, terms are often defined in one of the first sections of a bill. For the courts, the bill-drafter must try to anticipate constitutional or other grounds on which the bill, if enacted, might be challenged. Many state constitutions require that every bill enacted have a title, that it be limited to a single subject, and that it contain an enacting clause. The title facilitates communication by providing a brief identification of the bill and a list of statutory provisions (by number) that the bill would amend or repeal. While the single-subject limitation is intended to prevent confusion and to limit the possibility of a covert strategy (achieving one purpose under the cover of another purpose), determination of singleness or plurality of subject is judgmental and is dependent upon judicial attitude.

Still another aspect of the bill-drafter's technology is summarization; that is, listening to committee dialogue so that agreements on general and specific intentions can be expressed in the bill that the committee orders. (It is interesting, however, that preambles and other statements of intention are not considered binding by the courts. The courts reserve the right to interpret a law "on its face.")

Generally speaking, the sectioning of a bill follows the logic of establishing units of legislation that will facilitate future consideration of a problem proposal by components.

As in phase 1, the process of constructing a bill reveals the legislative organization's dependence on components of the task environment. These dependencies are imperatives that the legislature must recognize. If the legislature does not anticipate the basic requirements of implementation and the grounds of litigation, both of which are conditions that stem from governmental activities beyond complete legislative control, its decisions will often be fruitless. Since these kinds of "influences" cannot be buffered, they must be accommodated, much as a manufacturing organization must take into account the factors that make some products unmerchandizable.[12]

The existence of the Revisor's Office, and the staff of lawyers that compose it, buffers the lawmaking technology from its dependence on outsiders for bill construction. And the staff makes it possible for the legislature to reduce the likelihood that enactments can be ignored or circumvented.

But the drafting of a bill serves more than the purpose of limiting dependence on the environment. The bill facilitates all stages of the technology that follow. In general, a bill transforms a proposal for resolving or managing a problem into a communicable statement that can then be considered in whole or in part and that can be accepted or rejected in whole or in part. The importance of a bill as a tool in the legislative technology comes into bold relief when one imagines what would happen if proposals lacked the uniformity and specificity that bills provide. Chaos would obviously result.

This summary description and brief analysis of the bill-construction phase of the legislative technology would be incomplete without reference to the variety of such bills, not with regard to subject matter, but with respect to length, comprehensiveness, and comprehensibility. The uniformities of bills do not preclude the employment of strategies, initially or subsequently, strategies such as deliberate ambiguity, obfuscation, or concealment. Strategic considerations provide one explanation for the variation in bills. Other explanations include the idiosyncratic behavior of legislators and technological failure resulting from lack of skill or overdemands during peak periods. The last of these organizational problems is endemic in state legislatures, perhaps primarily because of the severity of time constraints.

Phase 3: Committee Action

The most general attributes of the legislature's dominant technology, as described so far, are considering and transforming—deciding whether to treat a problem legislatively and then transforming the problem proposal into a manageable instrument. The most consistent feature of the second of these sequential activities is that it is anticipatory, answering basic questions.

The third stage of the technology may be described as "winnowing" or "screening"—that is, deciding which bills should be reported unfavorably and which bills should be brought to the Committee of the Whole. The winnowing process really begins when House and Senate leaders decide to which committees bills should be referred. Committee action may be guided (sometimes predetermined) when leaders assign certain bills to committees whose chairmen or members are responsive to the wishes of the leadership. This kind of screening is less likely to occur in the United States House of Representatives or in any other legislature where the assignment of bills is governed by rules, that is, is regularized.

The formalized and visible screening occurs in committees. Bills that are perceived as being undesirable or not critical are killed by unfavorable reports or by shelving. It has been estimated that only 10 percent of the bills that are introduced will be passed during the same session in which they are introduced. Sometimes, unfavorable action on a bill is delayed because a committee member favors the bill. The norm of courtesy provides such a bill slightly more consideration than it would otherwise receive.

In Kansas, committee procedure is essentially ungoverned by formal rules, but certain uniform practices are observable:

1. Hearings are conducted on controversial proposals, usually when requested by one or more legislator-sponsors or by organized interest groups. Customarily, one time segment is allocated to proponents, and another to opponents.

2. Committees are staffed by a secretary (who prepares the minutes), by one or two analysts of the Legislative Research Department, and by a staff member of the Office of the Revisor of Statutes. Analyses of selected bills and other materials are prepared by staff at the direction of the chairman and sometimes the committee.

3. *Robert's Rules of Order* are treated as governing when procedural questions arise.

4. In general, dialogues in committees focus on the possible and probable consequences of bills, if enacted.

5. Bills deemed important are usually considered section by section before being reported favorably for passage.

6. In every session, standing committees develop their own bills, by having them drafted by staff and by passing assigned bills or by amending them to conform to the will of a majority of the committee members.

7. Standing committees during a session meet at scheduled times in assigned rooms unless the chairman calls a special meeting.

Aspects of committee procedure that are not uniform may be summarized as follows:

1. Some chairpersons maintain firm control of committee proceedings; others do not.

2. Some committees utilize staff services extensively; others do not.

3. Some chairpersons know and apply *Robert's Rules of Order*; some do not.

4. Some committees deliberate at length on many bills; others tend to act quickly.

5. Some committees solicit testimony; some do not.

The linkages of committees to groups in their task environments are most visible when hearings are conducted. The general practice of allowing interest groups to be heard during the screening process is not often violated. Representatives of the components of the task environment monitor committee meetings and are occasionally permitted to participate in discussions that are not treated as hearings.

Less visible linkages of committees to the environment are the interest-group memberships or backgrounds of committee members and the differential status of spokesmen for interest groups in their access to the chairman and individual committee members. The former is illustrated by the predominance of farmers on the Kansas House and Senate Committees on Agriculture and Livestock.

The screening process is a relatively unsystematic technology which is highly vulnerable to informal influences. Sets of alternative consequences are rarely identified in any organized manner. For example, the charismatic qualities of a member are relatively "unbuffered," and the recommendations of leaders are transmitted informally to chairmen and selected members.

Despite its unsystematic nature, screening is functionally necessary. Without it, the third phase of the dominant technology would be overloaded, given the time constraints of a legislative session and given the unlimited right of members to introduce bills and to participate in the agenda-building process. This phase of the process also poses the most difficult challenge in the assessment of technology, which is to counter the organization's vulnerability to the limited visions and special interests of one or a few of its members.

The institutional roles of a legislature, particularly with regard to the management of representation and conflict, preclude protection of the screening technology from the kinds of influences mentioned above. But adroit committee chairmen, armed with committee rules and staff support, can limit or prevent the reporting of shoddy products—bills that are poorly drawn or inadequately analyzed. In essence, this means the buffering of committee work from pressures that would sacrifice or impair good workmanship.[13]

Also, screening is functionally necessary, given the constraints of time and the principle of representation. Even in legislative bodies that limit the time allocated for debate on the floor, as in the United States House of Representatives, there is not enough time to allow floor debate on every bill that is introduced. American legislative organizations characteristically assign the screening activity to committees. To put severe limitations on the right of members to introduce bills might eliminate the necessity of screening, but such a measure would threaten the ability of legislators to perform the role expected of them—namely, the representation of their constituents.

Phase 4: Debate on General Orders

The projecting phase of a legislature's dominant technology occurs when the House and the Senate proceed as committees of the whole to debate bills on the general-orders section of the calendar.[14] The term "projecting" refers to the sharing of expectations with regard to various possible or probable consequences of a bill, if enacted. Nothing is implied about the motives, the intensity of belief, the objectivity, or the breadth and depth of the analytical efforts of the participants. What is asserted is that, in fact, most statements that are made while bills are being debated during the general-orders phase are projections of consequences and that this kind of analytical activity is logical, given the uncertainties attending the resolution and management of public problems and given the right of every member to vote on proposed legislation.

The legislative process is intended to be rational; that rationality is achieved in part by the sharing of judgments and information with respect to the possible effects of a lawmaking decision. It would make no sense to ask the members of a legislature to vote on each of the diverse kinds of bills that survive the screening process and to do so without benefit of knowing how the sponsors and other colleagues perceive the effects of a bill.

Consider how phase 4, debate on general orders, is structured. Beginning with the motion of the floor leader to convert the house into a committee of the whole for the purpose of considering bills on General Orders, a regularized series of events follows. The first bill is called up, and the member carrying that bill explains the bill, sometimes section by section, yielding for questions and comments, responding as he deems appropriate, acceding to or opposing amendments that may be moved to change the wording of a section, and after all who wish to be heard have been heard, making the closing argument and moving that the bill be recommended for final action and passage. The procedure is designed to permit clarification of the problem, articulation of the proposal, and projection of possible consequences and evaluation.

Whether, in fact, legislators are attentive to the arguments, weigh the pros and cons, and then make up their minds accordingly is a question. In any case, the dominant technology is constructed so as to permit and encourage them to do so; if it were not, the credibility and, ultimately, the survival of the legislature would be in jeopardy.

Though votes are taken during phase 4, the voting is not functionally necessary except on amendments. Otherwise, it would be possible to eliminate the aye and nay decisions on bills during the general-orders phase without jeopardizing the technology as a whole.

That is not to say, however, that the voting during the general-orders phase is useless. The votes perform a testing function. What is tested—imprecisely, unless a roll call is ordered—is the probability of passage when the bill is up for final action, when deciding occurs.

Though phase 4 is visible to anyone who wishes to watch and listen to the proceedings from the gallery, constituents' knowledge of what is said and by whom generally depends on what the members of the media and observers for interest groups report. The Kansas legislature enhances the opportunities of media representatives to observe and to report by providing them with access to the floor, a privilege that is denied to lobbyists and individual citizens. At the same time, the legislature buffers the influence of constituents by the rule that voice votes are taken unless a roll call is ordered. Except when roll-call votes are taken, individual legislators are generally able to preserve their anonymity, and thus their accountability for the positions that they have taken.

Phase 5: Final Passage

In a formal sense, the vote on final action of a bill is the act of *deciding*. It would constitute the moment that the legislative product is finished were it not for the possibility, sometimes the probability, that the product will be returned for further decision-making because of changes made by the second house or because of gubernatorial rejection.

The votes on final action are environmentally linked by the requirement that they be recorded. The function of accountability is served in a way that would not be true of the votes of a board of directors in a private corporation. Stockholders are rarely apprised of how board members vote on specific policy issues. The rule that permits members to explain their votes on the record formalizes the accountability function.

Unrecorded aye and nay voting buffers the influence that constituencies and interest groups have on organizational decision-making. This is one of the characteristics that distinguish the fourth and fifth phases of the legislature's dominant technology. During the fifth phase, every member present is required to "stand up and be counted."

The act of deciding does not reveal why individual members vote as they do. What is determined by the voting is the combined numerical weight of all the factors that cause members to vote aye or nay on a particular proposal at a particular time. Some of the many reasons for members' voting as they do are suggested by the following statements (not in order of importance): (1) Some members vote on the basis of their favorable or unfavorable perceptions of the bill's sponsor. (2) Some members will support the position of their political party if a position has been taken. (3) Some members accept the cues of those whose judgments they respect and whose interests they share. (4) Some members vote according to whether they perceive the proposal as consistent or inconsistent with their ideology or philosophy. These variations contribute to the ambiguity of legislative intent, an uncertainty that affects the emerging technology (the overseeing of executive operations) and all who are involved in the implementation of the laws that the legislature enacts.

The projecting phase of the legislature's dominant technology occurs when the House and the Senate proceed as committees of the whole to consider bills and resolutions on general orders. The technological significance of this activity would be relatively easy to specify if debate on general orders primarily served the function that it is purported to serve, namely, a marshaling of all arguments that may be made to persuade or dissuade members from voting for a bill or amendments to the bill. But the often-expressed judgment of experienced legislators that it is relatively unusual for debate to determine the fate of a bill suggests that debate on general orders serves purposes other than rational persuasion (such as consideration of a bill on its merits).

Phase 6: Conference Committees

The sixth phase occurs when a bill is returned to the house of origin because the other house has passed the bill after making minor or major changes in the bill. The choices open to the members in the house of origin are (1) to concur in the amendments, (2) not to concur, and (3) if not concurring, to assent to the appointment of a conference committee. If a conference committee is appointed and it subsequently reports back to the house, the members may then decide whether to accept or reject the conference committee's report. In the Kansas legislature, reports of conference committes are not amendable under the rules; therefore, rejection of a report constitutes final action unless the members call for a new conference committee.

The essence of this phase of the technology includes bargaining and compromise, but the latter is descriptive only if the bill is sent to the governor's desk. The failure of the two houses to agree on a single version of a bill represents the failure of efforts to bargain successfully, that is, to achieve a compromise.

The activities of legislative leaders are critically important during this phase of the lawmaking process. Though this observation will be treated more completely in chapter 7, on the role of leadership, it should be noted here that the influence of elements in the task environment at this stage will depend on the perceptions and actions of the leaders. The leaders appoint the members of the conference committees and are therefore in a potentially strong position to control or affect the products.

Bargaining is functionally necessary because of the bifurcated structure of most legislatures and because of the constitutional requirement that, to be enacted, a bill must be passed by both houses in identical form.

Phase 7: Gubernatorial Vetoes

The essence of the final stage, the decision to override or not to override a governor's veto, is *confrontation*. The veto holds unless there is a consensus of the members that the governor's position should not prevail; in the Kansas legislature, consensus is defined as agreement of two-thirds of the members in each house voting separately.

The task environment in this phase contains the constituents perceived as party identifiers or independents. If the governor belongs to the party opposed to the one that holds a majority of the legislative seats, confrontation will tend to be an interparty showdown. It will also tend to be a party contest if most Republicans vote differently from most Democrats, even when the party of the governor and the legislative majority are the same.

In traditional democratic theory, party confrontation is viewed as functional, as serving the principle of accountability; that is, it clarifies the policy choices for the voters in a manner that permits them ultimate influence on legislative outputs.

The inputs into a legislative organization's dominant technology occur in the considering or agenda-building phase. The outputs are the laws that are enacted when the governor signs the bills and/or when the legislature overrides a gubernatorial veto. Transforming, screening, projecting, and bargaining are the principal attributes of the phases that occur sequentially between the beginning and the ending.

Overall, the dominant technology is an analytical-judgmental technology that is uneven in its regularity and predictability, uneven in the influence of the components of the task environment, and uneven in the extent to which the legislative organization has been able to buffer those influences. Perhaps the best explanation of the unevenness lies in the uncertainties that legislatures face, a condition that is more characteristic of legislative organizations than of most other kinds of complex organizations in the United States.

PART 2

What has been described is a rational process of transforming inputs into outputs that is more or less characteristic of lawmaking in all American legislatures. But though it is rational—that is, instrumental to the lawmaking purpose for which legislatures exist—it is not the only way this technology could be constructed. Why, then, do most legislatures proceed in this fashion? To say that it is traditional, that most constitution builders and the first state legislators copied what the Congress and its predecessors devised, is at best a partial explanation. Given the proclivity of Americans for institutional innovation, why has the process of lawmaking remained relatively unchanged?

The answer to this question is to be found in certain characteristics of a legislature that differentiate it from other kinds of complex organizations, characteristics that are externally imposed and are not subject to major internal modifications.[15]

Consider together the following two characteristics: (1) *In contrast to centrally regulated, hierarchically structured organizations, authority in legislatures resides in the membership.* (2) *In contrast to most organizations in the private sector, the members are not hired by the leaders; their participation is contingent upon the support of constituents who are organized into electoral districts, support that is determined by periodic elections.* The most obvious effects of these characteristics are that leaders are elected and that debating and voting are primary activities in the lawmaking technology. Even if the members were willing to delegate to the leaders the power to decide issues of policy and to retain for themselves only a ratifying role, accountability to constituents would virtually preclude such a sweeping delegation of power. Thus, these characteristics of the legislature as an organization explain much of the lawmaking procedure and serve to limit the options in changing the technology.

Though these externally imposed characteristics would not prevent the members from depriving the leaders of all power, maintenance of the technology prevents serious consideration of this kind of major innovation. That argument will be explained in chapter 6.

The outer boundaries of technological change are relatively clear, but the latitude for innovation remains undefined. For example, would it be feasible to eliminate debate on general orders and to replace this phase with some other system for exchanging information?

Though this question is difficult to answer in the absence of knowledge of how such an alternative would work, it is apparent that a symbolic aspect of modern legislatures would be jeopardized. Whether realistically or not, legislatures are still perceived as debating forums, even though in Congress relatively few members are on the floor when debates occur. But congressional practice in this respect is a much less viable alternative for the Kansas legislature because of another characteristic: (3) *Membership activities are part time; the livelihood of the members depends on occupations outside the legislative organization.* The most immediate effects of this condition are that the legislature operates under severe time constraints and that the turnover of membership is relatively high. The trade-off is maintenance of the concept of a citizen legislature; that is, citizens have the opportunity to serve who would not if the position required their full time every year.

The time constraints reinforce whatever other arguments may be made for the third stage of the dominant technology, the screening process. The number of bills that are introduced in the agenda-building phase must be limited to the number that can be considered by the whole membership within the time allotted for a legislative session. Even if limitations were not put on the right of members to introduce bills, another characteristic would (given the time constraint) require a screening or winnowing procedure: (4) *With one exception, state legislative organizations are bicameral. Two organizations perform the same technologies which are linked by the constitutional requirement that they concur if the goals of either are to be achieved.* This feature, which is so uncharacteristic of other complex organizations, necessitates the adjustments and accommodations that occur in phase 6, that of conference committees. The bargaining made necessary by the bicameral structure could be eliminated by the adoption of a constitutional change to a unicameral legislature, which, in turn, would decrease the points of access to individuals and interest groups. But it would not fundamentally change another characteristic of legislative organization: (5) *Though all organizations are dependent upon environment, the dependence of a legislature on components of the task environment in the operation of its dominant technology is greater than in other organizations.* Market conditions, the availability and cost of raw materials and skilled labor, consumer needs and wants, and competition—all are environmental conditions that affect the operation of manufacturing organizations; but their leaders can buffer these influences in different ways and can retain relative freedom to construct and modify their technologies in order to enhance the organization's goals. In contrast, outside groups participate in or otherwise affect the legislative technology at all stages; the opportunities to buffer such influences are quite limited. The governor, executive-branch agencies, the courts, the press, interest groups, other levels of government, and constituents are all direct and indirect participants in the legislature's dominant technology.

The participation of nonlegislative groups in the lawmaking process, a factor that limits the number and kinds of procedural changes that could be made, stems from still another organizational characteristic: (6) *The outputs of a few organizations have as much impact on the environment as have those of legislatures.* Though bounded, the policy domains of legislatures are very broad, and they provide considerable latitude to these organizations in either narrowing or expanding the range of their impacts. Nonlegislative organizations usually enjoy much less flexibility in the contraction and expansion of their domains. Though constrained by constitutional rules (for example, federalism, the separation of powers, and bills of rights), legislatures can affect the lives of constituents in numerous ways.

Finally, another characteristic of legislative organizations helps the basic form of the dominant technology: (7) *Legislatures are expected to face and solve problems in an environment that does not fully disclose the alternatives that are available or the consequences of those alternatives.* Virtually all phases of the lawmaking process, cumbersome though they appear to be, make sense when viewed from this perspective. If alternatives and consequences could be maximized (à la the rational model of decision-making), satisficing would no longer be acceptable. And then the dominant technology could and would be modified considerably. But until we know more than we know presently, legislatures will have to live with uncertainty and with a technology that is an adjustment to that condition.

The argument of the second part of this chapter is that the relatively unchanged form of the lawmaking technology is explainable by the characteristics that distinguish legislatures from other kinds of complex organizations in the American society. Each phase of the dominant technology becomes rational when viewed from the perspective of organizational characteristics. These linkages do not preclude changes designed to improve the technology, but they do limit the options.

5
Overseeing:
The Emerging Technology

Overseeing the operations of agencies in the executive branch is an emerging, evolving technology in the Kansas legislature. The principal overseeing activities, which are shown in table 5.1, were all begun during the past twenty-five years. Although the Ways and Means committees and, intermittently, the other standing committees have inquired into agency operations throughout the history of the legislature, it was only recently that (1) a fiscal staff was added to the Legislative Research Department, (2) a law was enacted mandating legislative review of the rules and regulations formulated by state agencies to implement enactments, (3) the Division of Legislative Post Audit was organized, and (4) the Finance Council was created. In none of these four overseeing operations have routines developed that could be labeled "established."

Defining technology as what an organization does to achieve the purposes for which the organization exists directs attention to goals and objectives as well as to procedures. What are the ends to which the overseeing activities of the legislature are directed?

In the theory of separation of powers, each branch of government is expected to act as a check on the other branches. Montesquieu, to whom the Federalists attributed the theory of separation, argued that

TABLE 5.1

LEGISLATIVE OVERSEEING OF OPERATIONS IN THE EXECUTIVE BRANCH: AN OVERVIEW

Function	Instrument	Activities Scrutinized	Action
Fiscal review	Ways and Means committees, assisted by the fiscal staff of the Legislative Research Department	Budgetary policy decisions and revenue estimates	Agenda items prepared
Review of rules and regulations	Standing committees, assisted by staff of the Revisor's Office	Rules and regulations formulated by executive agencies to implement enactments	Approval or rejection
Performance audits	Post Audit Committee, assisted by staff of the Division of Legislative Post Audit	Agency compliance; program efficiency and effectiveness	Investigative reports (findings and recommendations)
Review of appropriations and personnel modification	State Finance Council	Proposals for changes in appropriations and for amendments to personnel system	Authorize actions to be taken by agencies

liberty cannot be secure if there exists in society any unrestrained power, that power can only be restrained by power, and that power must be set against power within the structure of government.[1] Though in American government it is more accurate to say that the separate institutions share power than to say that powers are separated, the fact remains that Americans expect the legislative, executive, and judicial branches to act as checks and balances on one another. In that context the legislative overseeing of executive operations is a means of discharging a "watchful" or "control" responsibility. Fact-finding and investigative activities are thought to be necessary and proper, whether or not any corrective measures are taken in consequence of what is learned.

A less inferential and more specific constitutional function of legislatures is to levy taxes and allocate resources. That responsibility alone justifies the legislative overseeing of executive operations. Only as legislatures become aware of how programs are working can they decide rationally which programs should be continued or which programs should be strengthened and how. Scarce resources and proliferating public problems intensify a legislature's need for the kinds of information that bureaucracies can supply. But to obtain information, legislatures have found it necessary to initiate inquiries and to develop structures and procedures to that end.

The fact that legislatures create executive-branch agencies and are constitutional participants in decisions regarding reorganization provides another justification for their overseeing activities. Independence of judgment in this category of decision-making requires review methods that will not be easily skewed by interests of the executive branch.

Though all of the overseeing activities that occur in the pursuance of these goals may be considered agenda-building, and therefore extensions of the lawmaking technology, they are separable because of their special relationship to maintenance of the legislature's institutional integrity and autonomy. Years ago it became apparent that legislatures that were unable or unwilling to oversee the operations of the executive branch were often at the mercy of the executive branch. To extricate their institutions from that condition, legislators began to develop techniques of overseeing. Together these methods suggest an emerging technology.

What is required is to learn what should be known and how that "what" can be learned. Asking the right questions and utilizing the skills by which answers are obtained form the essence of the technology of overseeing. These questions underlie the descriptive-analytical exposition in part 1 of this chapter.

In part 2 the argument is made that there are patterns in bureaucratic behavior that need to be understood before the overseeing technology can be useful as a means of improving policy-making.

PART 1

Fiscal Review

It has always been the function of the legislature to appropriate funds for the operation of departments and agencies in the executive branch. In deciding how much money to appropriate for each agency, the legislature has exercised selective judgment—selective in the sense that particular programs and activities have been subjected to review during the committee and general-orders phases of the lawmaking process. Generally speaking, review occurred when committees or individual legislators undertook to appropriate more or less than the amounts recommended in the governor's budget. Under these circumstances, the legislature acted as an appeals court, evaluating pro and con arguments for increases and decreases. Often the appeals process began and ended in the Ways and Means committees; but in every session, one or more issues were raised during general-orders debate on appropriations bills when efforts were made to amend the bills.

These reviews of agency operations were ad hoc, unsystematic, and generally unsupported by any kind of fact-finding that could be characterized as in-depth analyses. They resulted from initiatives on the part of an agency or a legislator when either or both parties were disquieted by the amounts of money recommended or by the nature of the programs or activities affected.

The unpredictable aspect of these legislative "reviews" began to change gradually as the legislature consciously moved to enhance its overseeing performance. First, the chairmen of the Ways and Means committees, or their designated representatives, were authorized by legislation to attend the governor's budget hearings, so that they would be more knowledgeable about agency operations and the governor's budgetary decisions. Second, the Ways and Means committees began to organize themselves into subcommittees for the purpose of reviewing agency budgets. Third, further specialization occurred when, by informal agreement, the Ways and Means committees of the House and the Senate divided the agency budgets for review purposes.

All these procedures increased the legislature's capability of understanding aspects of executive-branch operations; but more importantly, these procedures provided the legislature with a degree of independence that has come to be associated with the idea of legislative overseeing. The Division of the Budget in the State Department of Administration, which is subject to the direction of the governor, began to serve as staff for both the governor and the Ways and Means committees. In practice, the committees were restricted to a reactive role. They could react to the same issues that the governor confronted; but without a staff of their own, they lacked the ongoing ability to develop their own issues or to review those policy decisions embedded in the budget that did not surface in the governor's hearings on agency budgets.

The consciousness of legislative dependence on the governor and on agencies accountable to the governor became evident years ago, but it was during the administration of Governor Robert Docking that legislative leaders first decided to create a fiscal staff, hired by the legislature, to serve the Ways and Means committees and, in general, to provide the legislature with an independent capability for reviewing the budget.[2]

Today the fiscal staff seeks to identify the critical decisions made during the budgetary process, decisions that may or may not have come to the governor's attention. This analytical-judgmental activity is based on the premises that (1) every agency budget, and particularly the budgets of major agencies, contains one or more policy issues that ought to be brought to the attention of members of the Ways and Means committee; (2) information relevant to these issues should be collected and organized in advance of the time that the committees consider the appropriations bills; and (3) critical decisions will not be obvious to anyone who may read agency budgets, however carefully. The staff does not assume that executive budgets are deliberately concealing, but rather that budget documents are based on premises that are not articulated, premises involving policy decisions that ought to be known to legislative policy-makers.

An example is provided by the budgets of the state universities and colleges, in which unclassified and classified positions are allocated according to a formula based primarily on enrollment. The formula represents a policy decision that legislators may wish to accept or modify. There may be reasons for the formula to be reviewed, but a review is not likely in the absence of the kind of analytical work that the fiscal staff can provide.

An example of an executive budgetary decision that legislators are likely to want to review *every* year is the estimate of state general revenues. In Kansas, the revenue estimate is a decision of considerable importance, given the constitutional prohibition of deficit financing. Since the projection of revenues is not an exact science, income expectations will vary, and they can also be influenced by political interests. (The independence of the legislature in determining the total amount of general-revenue funds that will be available for appropriation in any fiscal year would not exist in the absence of an ability to decide whether executive projections are too high, about right, or too low.) Today, in the special technology of revenue projection, staff members of the Legislative Research Department participate with the staff and consultants of the Department of Administration's Budget Division and the Department of Revenue. This shared activity of executive and legislative personnel facilitates legislative overseeing as well as potential agreement on the ceiling for spending.

Though virtually all of the activities of the fiscal staff serve the lawmaking process, they also facilitate the overseeing operations of the executive branch. If the overseeing function were not intended, there would be no compelling reason to create a fiscal staff. Hence, it is appropriate to treat the work of the fiscal staff as a part of the emerging technology.

Their work is *sequential*, in the sense that a part of what they do depends on and is geared to the budgetary cycle in the executive branch. But it is also *intensive*, because they decide what to analyze and because decisions of the Ways and Means committees will depend in part on their findings.

Through the activities of the fiscal staff the legislature buffers its dependence on the governor and executive agencies in appropriating public monies. At the same time, aspects of agency operations are brought under legislative scrutiny.

It is probably too early to predict how intensively and extensively agency operations will be examined by the fiscal staff in the future, but legislators are becoming more conscious of the long-range fiscal impacts of the decisions that they make regarding appropriations. This concern is likely to encourage expansion of legislative inquiries into the manner in which agencies of the executive branch discharge their responsibilities and into the successes and failures of existing governmental programs.

Review of Rules and Regulations

The notion that agencies of the executive branch do not make policy decisions, that they merely carry out or implement policy decisions made by the governor and legislature, is no longer fashionable in the literature of public administration. Scholars today generally believe that agency personnel are involved in the formulation of public policy, not only by contributions to agendas relating to policy, but in the implementation of laws as well.

The first step in implementation is the preparation of rules and regulations governing the application of statutory provisions. Because rules and regulations are interpretative and because interpretations of a law may vary, sometimes considerably, the development of rules and regulations is considered to be an important policy-making function exercised by executive agencies. Recognition of that view by Kansas legislators led to the modification of a statutory provision governing that process, a modification designed to permit the legislature to modify or reject new or old rules and regulations.

In effect, the Kansas legislature exercises a veto power with respect to all changes in existing or new rules and regulations. To the extent that the legislature exercises that power through the Joint Committee on Administrative Rules and Regulations or through subject-matter committees, the legislature performs an overseeing function.

The procedure that has evolved to this point may be summarized as follows:

1. After an agency has filed proposed modifications of existing or new rules and regulations with the Revisor's Office, the proposals are submitted to the Joint Committee, which, in the case of new rules, may recommend rejection or modification by a concurrent resolution or, in the case of old rules, may draft a bill to express the changes that the committee desires.

2. Any bill proposed by the Joint Committee will be referred to the appropriate standing committees.

3. The chairman or subcommittee chairman then asks the agency administrator to explain the new rules or amendments or to respond to the Joint Committee's actions.

4. Finally, the standing committees decide whether to approve, modify, or reject the bill introduced by the Joint Committee.

Through this procedure the Kansas legislature attempts to ensure that the first stage in the implementation of laws is consistent with the legislature's intent.

Martha Derthick, author of *The Influence of Federal Grants*, contends that the conditions attached to federal grants are the best source of information about federal goals and objectives.[3] The conditions translate statements of legislative purpose, which are often ambiguous and general, into explicit goals. Those kinds of policy statements are generally necessary if an enactment is to be implemented. At the same time, they represent extensions of legislative policy-making. Whether they are consistent with legislative intent (as legislative overseers understand it) is a question that legislators dare not fail to ask if the preeminence of the legislative organization in policy-making is to be maintained. Review of rules and regulations is a means of preserving that preeminence. It is a critical aspect of the emerging technology of overseeing.

Performance Audits

Postaudit operations may be described as *investigative* and *intensive*. The use of the term "intensive" calls attention to the fact that performance of program audits occurs only when the members of the Legislative Post Audit Committee decide that an audit should be conducted and because each audit is unique in certain respects. The nature of the concerns of the committee shapes the focus of the audit. Moreover, the kinds of analyses made by the postaudit staff also depend on the characteristics of the agency operations that are being examined. Thus, the uniformities observable in the lawmaking process are somewhat less likely to appear in successive program audits.

Agency audits are procedurally similar to program audits. In addition, the law mandates a financial audit for every state agency at least once every two years. But the term "intensive" is descriptive of this process as well, because each audit is independent of all other audits. A financial audit of one agency does not necessarily precede the audit of any other agency. The procedure by which an audit is conducted is, however, sequential. Auditors develop a step-by-step operation that is generally applicable in all agency audits. The result is an auditing technology that is standardized and understandable—at least to auditors. Moreover, the objective remains constant: agency audits are conducted so as to ensure agency accountability to those laws that regulate the handling of public monies. Increasingly, however, these audits, like program audits, include issues of efficiency and effectiveness. The usual coverage and content of reports on agency audits and program audits are shown in figure 5.1.

Program audits are intended to measure efficiency and effectiveness. "Measure" may be an inappropriate term, given the normative nature of those standards and the imprecision of the tests used to determine efficiency and effectiveness. The meaning of this distinction between agency audits and program audits becomes more understandable when the events of a program audit are described.

A program audit begins with the concerns of the Legislative Post Audit Committee. When the members think an inquiry (audit) should be made, and they direct the staff to do so, the program-audit technology is triggered. The next step in the process is to transform the committee's concerns into audit objectives that in one way or another are researchable. What follow are the information-gathering decisions, formulation of a strategy to obtain data and knowledge that will be relevant to the objectives. Since information-gathering involves a limited number of options—examination of documents and records, interviews, questionnaires, and on-site inspections—all program audits appear to be similar at this stage. The variations will depend on the availability of information in printed form and on assessments of the objectivity of that information. The strategy also

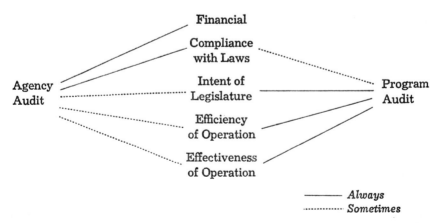

FIGURE 5.1: LEGISLATIVE DIVISION OF POST AUDIT: ELEMENTS OF THE AUDIT

includes a decision about what constitutes a basis of comparison, because comparison is the essential analytical activity by which judgments of efficiency and effectiveness are made. The results of that analysis emerge at the next stage, which involves determinations of findings. Then follows the development of recommendations, the deductive task of drawing out what is implied in the findings. And finally, closure occurs when the Post Audit Committee decides what, if anything, to do about the findings and recommendations of the staff.

This general description of a program audit glosses over the differences between efficiency and effectiveness as goals. In judging efficiency, the overriding question is whether the program's operation of an agency could be performed at less cost in resources without sacrificing the objectives of the program. Since efficiency is generally considered to be a responsibility of management, program audits often include an analysis of the agency's management. In analyzing management, postauditors in Kansas begin with the assumption that good management requires (1) the setting of measurable objectives, (2) the development and maintenance of an informational network, (3) formulation of systematic policies and procedures, and (4) the application of performance indicators. Failure to perform any of these tasks is viewed as a weakness in management and an actual or potential explanation for inefficiency.

The use of effectiveness as a criterion raises the question of how well a given program addresses the problem(s) for which the program was inaugurated or for which it exists. By this standard it is appropriate to ask, for example, whether a program to eradicate noxious weeds is in fact eradicating noxious weeds. It is theoretically possible that an operation that is judged to be inefficient may nonetheless be judged effective.

Obviously, all programs are not as researchable with regard to effectiveness as is the program for eradication of noxious weeds. The decline in the presence of bindweed may be a quantifiable finding, and this may be attributable to an agency's application of herbicides. In contrast, how is the effectiveness of a welfare program to be measured? The analytical task of specifying measures for this kind of program can be a difficult undertaking.

It is generally assumed that legislative intent provides postauditors with guidelines in assessing program effectiveness; that is, the substandards of the measures employed are assumed to be explicit or implicit in the enactment that brought the program into being. But in fact, determining legislative intent is often difficult and sometimes impossible.

Table 5.2 illustrates a program audit. It was compiled from a report entitled *Regulating the Appropriation and Use of Water*, which was issued on 8 December 1975. It is particularly revealing of failures by both the legislature and agencies in the executive branch in protecting water rights and in conserving water. It also brings into sharp focus a limitation of the overseeing technology—the possibility, perhaps even the probability, that nothing will happen in spite of an extensive investigation. If either the Post Audit Committee or other committees fail to act on recommendations and the executive agencies then behave accordingly, if rank and file legislators do not read the audit reports and then consider appropriate action, or if the governor does not employ his administrative and legislative powers to this end, a postaudit investigation becomes a symbolic rather than a substantive exercise in legislative overseeing.

In making this observation we do not mean to imply that every program audit ought to produce either legislative or executive actions, since some investigations yield findings for which no viable options exist or for which no action is believed necessary. But it is important to assess the outputs and outcomes of technologies as well as the logic of the procedures employed.

Appropriations and Personnel Modification Review

The State Finance Council is a somewhat controversial, hybrid suborganization of the Kansas legislature.[4] It is hybrid in the sense that one of its nine members is the governor (the other eight are legislators) and in the sense that its functions are mixed. Some observers think that it makes both legislative and executive kinds of decisions. Because of its composition and because of its powers, the council is periodically besieged as its critics challenge its constitutionality or introduce bills designed to terminate its existence.

But however controversial, the Finance Council is, in certain of its activities, an instrument by which certain operations of the executive branch are reviewed. It is appropriate, therefore, to include both a description of the council's activities as a part of a discussion of the overseeing activities of the legislature and, for what light it may shed on the nature of the council, a brief history of the council.

The predecessor of the council, the State War Emergency Fund Board, was not intended to be an overseeing instrument of the legis-

TABLE 5.2
REGULATING THE APPROPRIATION AND USE OF WATER

Reason for Audit	Objectives of Audit	Strategy of Audit	Findings of Audit	Recommendations of Audit
Increasing concern over declining water levels in central and western Kansas and the potential impact on the state of such declines.	1. Determine whether adequate information is available and being used by decision-makers on the safe yield and current use of the state's water resources 2. Examine the process of granting appropriation rights to determine compliance with statutes and regulations 3. Evaluate the state's ability to enforce statutes prohibiting unlawful use, allocation according	Survey activities of the Division of Water Resources for a ten-year period: (a) examine sources of data; (b) interpret data by use of statistically valid samples; (c) interview agency personnel	1. Diversionary works may be constructed and water may be used without first obtaining a permit from the chief engineer. This limits his ability to control, conserve, and regulate the state's water resources 2. The state engineer may establish rules and regulations clarifying a complex act, but he has not done so 3. The data on availability and use of water has not been collected, combined, and analyzed in a way that is useful for making decisions about the appropriation and use of water 4. The user and the state need accurate information in order to protect water	1. That it be unlawful to construct a diversionary work or use water for other than domestic purposes without permission from the chief engineer, and that all who use water should be required to obtain a permit within a specified period 2. That the Groundwater Protection Act be amended to prohibit a licensed well-drilling contractor from constructing a well unless a permit exists 3. That the chief engineer establish rules and regulations to clarify and interpret the act so that the water user can understand what impairment is and when a right is being impaired 4. That the Division of Water Resources request that the data collected on the availability, use, and quality of surface water and ground water be combined by

to priority of right, and identification and
termination of
abandoned water
rights

rights

5. Impairment of water
rights "seems to be occur-
ring" throughout the state,
but the lack of standards
defining impairment
makes it difficult to
prevent

6. There is a lack of in-
formation as to safe yield

the Board of Water Resources,
by the Department of Health
and Environment, and by the
Kansas Geological Survey for
purposes of water management
and administration of rights

5. That the chief engineer require all nondomestic users to
install water meters in order to
provide accurate information on
annual water use

6. That the chief engineer
develop sufficient information on
safe yield and existing use so
that he can properly evaluate
all applications

lature. It was originally created in 1943 to administer a state war-emergency fund. The members were empowered to make allocations and to authorize expenditures by state agencies for the purposes of protecting persons and property from dangers arising out of the war and for the purpose of repairing or replacing buildings and equipment damaged "by acts of God." In 1947 the board was continued by an enactment that deleted references to wartime conditions and powers.

The present State Finance Council was created in 1953 and was given functions that extend beyond those exercised by the State Emergency Fund Board. From time to time, additional duties and responsibilities were mandated, so that by the beginning of the 1976 legislative session the council exercised the following statutory powers:

1. To approve all rules and regulations proposed by the State Department of Administration

2. To authorize the State Board of Treasury Examiners to issue certificates of indebtedness

3. To hear and determine appeals by any state agency regarding decisions of the secretary of administration or the director of computer services

4. To make allocations to, and approve expenditures by, a state agency from any appropriations to the Finance Council of funds for unanticipated and unbudgeted needs

5. To fix or approve the compensation to be paid to a large number of officers and employees in the executive branch

6. To approve memorandum agreements resulting from labor negotiations

7. To approve assignment to classes of all positions in the classified exempt service

8. To approve salary schedules for state employees

9. To adopt an allocation system when it appears that monies in the General Revenue Fund will be insufficient to cover appropriations

10. To authorize transfers and expenditures of public monies under certain conditions

Following a decision of the Kansas Supreme Court, filed on 6 March 1976, the legislature amended the statutes. In an effort to comply with the court's rulings, certain of the powers listed above were relinquished. Subsequently, the attorney general of Kansas filed a second suit, alleging that, notwithstanding the 1975 amendments, the statutory provisions contravened the separation-of-powers principle in the Kansas Constitution. The Shawnee County District Court granted the petition of the plaintiff. The decision was appealed to the Kansas Supreme Court, which, on 14 March 1977, entered an order reversing the ruling of the lower court. As a consequence of this latest Supreme Court decision, the Finance Council, subject to legislative guidelines, may exercise the following powers:

1. The power to increase an expenditure limitation that is contained in an appropriation of special revenue funds
2. The power to authorize a state agency to exceed a limitation in expenditure of a reappropriated balance of an appropriation from the state's General Revenue Fund
3. The power to authorize a state agency to exceed a limitation imposed by an appropriations act on the number of personnel positions that may be funded by the act
4. The power to authorize state agencies to receive and spend money from federal grants or other sources

Any authorization requested of the council may be subjected to a critical review by members of the council. In the process of review the council is legally obliged to ask questions expressed or implied by the guidelines amended into the statutes during the 1976 session. A summary of those guidelines, stated in question form, follows.

1. Is the request within the purview of the council as determined by legislative delegation?
2. Does the request result from an unforeseeable occurrence or an unascertainable effect of a foreseeable occurrence?
3. Will the requested action assist the state agency in attaining an objective or goal that bears a valid relationship to authorized powers and functions of the agency?
4. Would delay in acting on the request until the next legislative session in some way obstruct or interfere with attaining an authorized goal or objective of the agency?
5. Was the request rejected by the legislature in a preceding session?
6. If the request is for authorization to receive and expend federal or other funds, is the program for which the authorization is requested beneficial to the health and welfare of the people of the state?

7. Does the request imply a vested commitment that a future legislative enactment will provide additional state funds to achieve the purpose of the proposed program?

It is evident that the breadth of the powers and the mandates implied by the guidelines provide the legislators on the council with considerable latitude for inquiry into operations of the executive branch. Whether the council chooses to examine the requests and to probe for justification depends upon how the members perceive their role. Since the council meets only during the interim, time is a constraint only if the members choose to regard it as such.

A comparison of the proceedings of the Finance Council with the inquiries and investigations of standing committees yields only two differences of any consequence. First, the agenda of the Finance Council is initiated by agents of the executive branch; in contrast, committee reviews are initiated by legislators. Second, the Finance Council's scope of inquiry is limited by statutory provisions; committees are free to probe into virtually all aspects of agency operations.

The future of the Finance Council is less certain than that of any of the other overseeing instrumentalities of the legislature. That uncertainty stems from its character as a "little legislature" and not because the council examines and dissects the plans and proposals of agencies. If the council survives further constitutional or legislative challenges, it is possible that the legislative members of the council will begin to feed back to standing committees some of the information that they acquire, information that may be relevant to the lawmaking responsibilities that committees are charged to perform. The minutes of the council must be provided to all legislators, but minutes may not convey the insights that members of the council may acquire during council interrogation of those who request authorizations.

To sum up, the subdominant technologies of the Kansas legislature are those that have evolved and are evolving to help the legislature oversee operations of agencies of the executive branch. Assessments of these activities should take into account that they are technologies in the making, rather than established and institutionalized processes. Finally, overseeing activities are linked to the dominant technology, the lawmaking process. If the legislature fails to oversee effectively, this will weaken its ability to make policy decisions that will safeguard and enhance the public's interests.

PART 2

The overseeing of the operations of the executive branch, the emerging technology, is in an early stage of development in the Kansas legislature. Three of the four organized overseeing activities described in the first part of this chapter were begun during the last decade. The ways in which this technology evolves will depend on how assiduously and systematically the principals—the legislators and the staff—endeavor to understand bureaucratic behavior. This proposition is based on the assumption that bureaucratic behavior can be patterned, that there are certain tendencies that are characteristic of bureaucracies, irrespective of the kinds of services they deliver. If this premise is sound, then it follows that legislative understanding of these patterns will inevitably affect the shaping of legislation. In the drafting and modification of bills, more attention will be given to their implementation, particularly when legislators are intent on addressing certain public problems substantively as well as symbolically.

What do we know about bureaucratic behavior? Have scholars been able to identify uniformities in bureaucratic behavior, patterns that are characteristic of executive-branch agencies generally?

Paradigms of bureaucratic behavior have been formulated, but there have been few empirical studies in which these models have been tested and applied. One of the best efforts to synthesize scholarship in this area of inquiry is Graham Allison's construction of the organizational process in his *Essence of Decision*.[5] In an effort to understand the policy recommendations made during the Cuban Missile Crisis to the president and to his staff by administrators in the Department of Defense, Allison pieced together perceptions of organizational tendencies. His general propositions indicate that policy-makers are well advised to be aware of the organizationally based biases and limitations of policy recommendations made by agents of bureaucratic structures.

From Allison's synthesis a number of propositions may be extracted to demonstrate the relevance of knowledge about bureaucratic behavior to legislative overseeing. Allison's contentions follow:

1. Agencies develop standard operating procedures and programs. The standard operating procedures are routines for dealing with standard situations. Programs are clusters of standard operating pro-

cedures. These repertoires include organizational priorities and perceptions that are relatively stable.

2. When agencies are mandated to carry out a policy decision that requires new activities, they tend to respond by making marginal adaptations to existing programs and activities. If incremental changes are not viewed as administratively feasible, they will create a subunit in order to attend to the policy requirement.

3. When a policy assignment is contrary to existing organizational goals, an agency tends to resist implementation of it.

4. Agencies rationalize their responses to policy directives and, in doing so, present incomplete and distorted information.

5. When agencies are asked to present alternative proposals to the policy-makers during the initial process of policy formulation, their menu of alternatives that are defined in sufficient detail to be live options will be severely limited in number and character.

6. Agencies are deficient in their ability to coordinate with other agencies regarding programs requiring coordination. Such projects are rarely accomplished according to design.

7. Long-range planning by agencies is usually a gesture. Planning is institutionalized, then disregarded.

8. Agencies tend to define the health of the organization in terms of budget, manpower, and territory rather than on the basis of program effects or impacts.

9. Programs, once undertaken, are not dropped at the point where objective costs outweigh the benefits. Organizational momentum easily carries them beyond the point of loss.

10. Organizations are not impervious to directed change, but this is not likely to occur unless there is a careful targeting of the major functions that support routines, such as personnel, rewards, information, and budgets.[6]

If these propositions are accepted as being fairly accurate generalizations, then it is evident that a considerable gap may separate what the policy-makers choose and what the agencies implement. And it follows that legislators dare not assume that what they mandate will be carried out automatically.

Unfortunately, recognition of that fact often leads legislators to perceive agencies as being devious, deceitful, and willfully disregarding of legislative mandates. This negative perception is not usually helpful as a diagnosis; it fails to take into account Allison's observation that organizations are blunt instruments, that inflexibility is the nature of the beast.

The problems of implementation become both preventable and manageable when legislators and their staff begin to anticipate these problems and hedge against them. This capability is achieved, not by adoption of specific prescriptions (which are generally unavailable), but by understanding acquired through overseeing inquiries. With present staff resources—however minimal—and consciousness of the potential assistance to policy formulation that overseeing activities can provide, the emerging technology should evolve into a fairly sophisticated legislative tool.

The argument of the second part of this chapter is that the postulate of bureaucratic tendencies should be accepted, at least tentatively, for the direction it provides in overseeing the operations of the executive branch.[7]

Awareness of implementation problems and their relevance to lawmaking, however, does not address some of the fundamental problems that Morris S. Ogul identified in *Congress Oversees the Bureaucracy*.[8] In this synthesizing and original study, Professor Ogul directed attention to the motivation and the stimuli to oversee, to the organizational means of performing the role of overseeing, and to the barriers to improvement of the performance of overseeing. With respect to the first, Ogul found that the members of Congress who give low priority to overseeing are apt to dislike their committee assignments and to perceive overseeing as having a low political salience.[9] With respect to the second, Ogul observed that the committee and subcommittee chairmen who have great influence over the fate of bills are best able to achieve overseeing goals if they are disposed to that end,[10] that increasing staff size does not necessarily lead to better overseeing,[11] and that the reorganization acts of 1946 and 1970 set excessive expectations for overseeing.[12] With respect to the third, Ogul concluded that "as long as the Congress is bicameral and the committees in each house are unwilling to coordinate with their counterparts in the other house, and as long as there are numerous standing committees and subcommittees in both houses with relative freedom to go their own way in investigating problems, the conduct of oversight will be difficult to alter substantially."[13] In addition, the constituency orientation of legislators, the fact that they get reelected for reasons other than their activities related to overseeing, is an obstacle to the improvement of overseeing.[14]

The problems that impede the development of performance with regard to overseeing in the Congress are likely to affect the evolution of the overseeing technology in the Kansas legislature. The difficulties will be compounded by the fact that the members are only part-time legislators. But the first steps have been taken: organizational mechanisms for overseeing have been created, and Kansas legislators are being made aware of overseeing as a legitimate and appropriate function of the legislature.

6
The Role of Leadership: Managing the Technologies

Legislative leaders are the managers of the legislative organization. They are responsible for maintaining the technologies of lawmaking and of overseeing the operations of the executive branch. Many of the decisions that they make are essentially managerial. They appoint staff directors; provide overall direction for staff activities; allocate positions, duties, and responsibilities to legislators as well as to staff; make budgetary decisions; and schedule decision-making events. As in all complex organizations, public and private, the administrative or managerial role is critical to achievement of goals and hence to survival of the organization.

Legislative leaders are not only institutional leaders; they also perform leadership roles in political parties. As party leaders they are expected to take care of party interests, to develop and to discover issue positions that most members of the party can support, and then to facilitate enactment of the bills that express those positions. Taking care of the party interests is platform-building, but it also entails the negative role of preventing the opposition party from achieving its platform-building objectives. As institutional leaders, leaders of the legislature are expected to define and articulate the mission of the legislature and to defend its integrity. In order to meet these expectations it usually becomes necessary for them to prevent transgressions of the limits of partisanship.

In practice, few legislative leaders distinguish among their managerial, party, and institutional roles, although these are analytically separable. By treating them as distinct sets of responsibilities, it is possible to understand the continuance of inefficiencies in the operation of legislative technologies as well as technological improvements and innovations. The three leadership roles are not always perceived as congruent.

In this chapter, the administrative, or managerial, role is the focus of part 1 (with occasional references to party and institutional roles where appropriate). The ways in which perceptions of party and institutional roles affect the performance of administrative and managerial roles are explored in part 2.

It should be noted at the outset that legislative organizations are atypical in that no single person administers the legislature as a whole, nor does any single person carry the burden of leadership alone.

Those who hold positions of authority with responsibilities that transcend the activities of a committee-level organizational unit are members of the Legislative Coordinating Council. By law, the council is composed of seven officers: the Speaker of the House of Representatives, the president of the Senate, the Speaker pro tem, the president pro tem, and the majority and minority leaders of both houses. This group of leaders shares important decision-making powers.

Outside the council, the duties and prerogatives of the leaders vary considerably. The Speaker exercises more authority in the House than the president exercises in the Senate, and the majority leaders in the House and Senate participate in the making of authoritative decisions that are not within the domain of the minority leaders, unless they are included by invitation.

The concept of leadership is sometimes defined by the criterion of influence; thus, members of an organization may be called leaders even though they hold no positions of authority. That broad meaning is not appropriate to this analysis, because it would require the authors to expand the scope of this book beyond its design. Formal position is a definition that is sufficient to the primary purpose of this chapter, which is to direct attention to an often-neglected aspect of legislative leadership: namely, the maintenance and improvement of technology.

PART 1

The Dominant Technology

Agenda-building. The interim committees have become the primary means by which the Kansas legislature considers problems and/or policy proposals. Most of the problems that the committees consider are assigned to them by the Coordinating Council, which winnows out many study requests in the process. The members of interim committees, as well as their chairmen, are selected by the council, initially by the majority-party members of the council. The minority-party members are given a voice in deciding which minority-party legislators shall serve on which interim committees, but the final decision is made by the majority members (in 1976 by the Speaker, the Speaker pro tem, the majority leader of the House, the president of the Senate, and the majority leader of the Senate). The council also decides how often interim committees may meet, and it allocates funds for special purposes.

While these decisions are being made, bargaining occurs between the House and Senate members of the council and occasionally between majority and minority members, because more legislators want to serve on particular interim committees than there are positions to be allocated. The conflict over assignments to interim committees would be more intense were it not for the fact that a few legislators do not want to serve on interim committees, and some are excluded because of a record of absenteeism.

In addition to making the decisions listed above, the council sets a deadline for submission of reports (by law, the first of December unless extended). The deadline is necessary in order to get the reports printed before the session begins in January.

This brief description of Coordinating Council decision-making identifies the kinds of decisions that must be made in the agenda-building phase. Obviously, not all of these decisions are equally important; the critical kinds are those in which it is decided to study certain problems and not others. Leaders justify their prerogative with the argument that they know by experience which proposals have been studied before, which proposals are potentially productive of needed legislation, and which ones reflect the interests of more than a few legislators. The bulk of study proposals submitted by legislators (two hundred were submitted during the 1976 session) are only suggestions to the leaders, who then decide which have sufficient merit for interim consideration. Two other sources of study proposals are the governor and standing committees. During every session, committees decide to defer issues or to carry over bills that they do not have time to examine thoroughly during that session. Some of these issues are assigned to interim committees. What makes all of these decisions critical is that they directly affect the legislative output of the next session.

No mention has yet been made of an important kind of agenda-building decision, one involving priority of proposals. When party leaders develop and announce a "program," they, in effect, give priority to certain proposals. During the last years of Governor Robert Docking's administration, the president of the Senate and the Speaker of the House announced their alternative to the governor's legislative program.

It is commonly believed that the setting of priorities is essential in order to ensure legislative consideration of the public's most urgent problems and that if priorities were not decided, important and sometimes indispensable actions would not be taken. It is also argued that the accountability function of the two-party system requires party programs.

Bill-drafting. In addition to their general supervisory responsibilities, legislative leaders must (1) recommend cutoff dates for the introduction of individual and committee bills (which dates have been included in the joint rules) and (2) direct the Revisor of Statutes Office to transform certain proposals of the governor into bills. It is also the responsibility of party leaders to (3) ensure the preparation and introduction of bills that express the party programs. The first of these functions is essential, given the time constraints of a session. The second is an appropriate courtesy, given the governor's constitutional mandate to present recommendations to the legislature each session. Whether the third function is necessary depends on how one perceives the priority-setting and party-program activities.

In the past, legislative leaders have also attempted to even out the work load of the Revisor's Office by urging legislators to prefile bills.

Committee action. The speaker of the Kansas House of Representatives selects the chairmen and vice-chairmen of standing committees, appoints the members of each committee, and assigns bills to committees. These three powers are nearly absolute. Ordinarily, the Speaker consults the minority leader in assigning committee positions to minority members, but he is not bound to honor his recommendations. The Speaker may also consult the majority leader and the Speaker pro tem, or any other member; but again, the appointment power is his to exercise.

It would be difficult to overemphasize the importance of the Speaker's power to appoint committee chairmen. By the choices he makes, the "quality" of committee actions is affected, if not determined. Through his appointees the Speaker can influence committee decisions, the expediting or delaying of reporting of bills, and the shaping of content. If he so chooses, the Speaker can set the guidelines for committees in the screening process. If he chooses to act in a partisan fashion, he can probably prevent bills that are authored by members of the minority party from being recommended for passage, or he can ensure that those same bills are reported out as committee bills. If one or more chairmen are inept, he must also accept some responsibility for this condition, though it is always difficult to remove a chairman.

In the Kansas Senate the chairmen and vice-chairmen of standing committees, as well as the members of those committees, are selected by the Committee on Organization, Calendar, and Rules, a committee that is composed of the president, the majority leader, and five members elected by the majority of the Senate. In the selection of members on standing committees, Senate Rule 7 requires that the minority party be given at least proportional representation. The assignment of bills to committees (reference) is the president's responsibility.

In the United States House of Representatives, bills are referred in a relatively routine manner, because precedents have established the jurisdiction of committees. That condition does not obtain in the Kansas legislature, where the Speaker and the president exercise considerable discretionary power in this respect. They can affect action on certain bills by the decisions they make regarding assignments. Double referral is used as a hedge against an unwanted bill or provision of a bill. Such a bill can then be sent to a second committee, there to die or be amended. In the House, the Committee on Federal and State Affairs has often served as the "Speaker's committee," the committee whose chairman and majority-party members are most amenable to the Speaker's leadership.

Whether the leaders ought to be able to influence the committee screening of bills in the manner described above is a debatable question. Strictly speaking, the dominant technology can work as long as the organizational and bill-referral decisions are made. The only other "power" of leaders at the committee stage that is essential to the lawmaking process is the ability to get some bills reported out early enough so that the calendar (for general orders) doesn't contain too few important bills at the beginning of the session and too many at the end of the session. "Traffic control" is a leadership function that is a technological necessity.

General orders. Determining the order of bills on the calendar is the essential decision-making responsibility of legislative leaders during the general-orders stage of the lawmaking process. For several reasons, it is not practical to call up bills for debate in the order in which they are reported out of committees. If that procedure were adopted, important bills would die on the calendar at the end of each session, because there is never enough time to debate all bills that have been reported favorably. The spacing of important bills would become a matter of chance rather than design. No allowances could be made for a member's lack of readiness to carry a bill. And the unwritten rule that "major bills stay on the calendar until there are enough votes to pass them" would have to be jettisoned. For all of these reasons, the Speaker of the House and the majority leader in the Senate control the calendar. Having control of the calendar indicates considerable power. The life and death of bills may depend on how the Speaker in the House and the majority leader in the Senate view both the sponsor and the content of the bills.

It is during the general-orders phase that party caucuses become important tools of the party leaders. The caucus may be used to test support or opposition to one or more bills, to achieve party cohesion, or both. Where leadership is strong, the caucus may serve as a means of communicating to party members what the party position is rather than as an arena for debating issues before they come to the floor.

Leadership "style" is reflected in the way that caucuses are used. When he served as majority leader in the United States Senate, Lyndon Johnson rarely called caucuses. Viewing caucuses as potentially divisive, he preferred instead to work with his colleagues on a one-to-one basis. In the Kansas legislature, Speaker McGill sent questionnaires to House members before a session began, a practice that gave him a reading on members' attitudes on major issues—information that, in his judgment, made caucuses useful only as a means of conveying party positions.

The Speaker of the House and the president of the Senate decide who will preside during general orders. This is an essential though relatively minor authority, except when highly controversial issues are up on the calendar. Under those circumstances the chairman of the Committee of the Whole can make parliamentary decisions that affect the fate of a bill. This is possible in the Kansas legislature because in neither chamber is there a parliamentarian who guides the chairman in deciding questions of procedure.[1] Procedural rules are only partly institutionalized, leaving room for discretion in the interpretation and application of rules.

The role of leaders in projecting the consequences of policy proposals, the primary function in the general-orders stage, is no more important than that of any member, except that leaders tend to be more conscious of potential political impacts than are other members. One kind of impact is what possible effect a decision will have on the prestige of the legislature. The role of testing support for and against proposals is essential for regulation of the calendar.

Final action. The primary function of leaders in the fifth stage of the lawmaking process (deciding) is to determine when it is essential to advance a bill to final action on the same day that it is reported favorably by the Committee of the Whole. Normally, a bill reported favorably by the committee is not on the calendar for final action until the succeeding day. In order to expedite action on bills, particularly during the final days of a session, it often becomes necessary to prevent the one-day delay. Otherwise the Senate and/or the House might not have time to act on the bill. This responsibility is a good example of what leaders must do to make the technology work.

The one-day delay may be used by leaders to try to influence members to change their minds and so ensure either passage or defeat of a bill. Though that same opportunity is open to all members, as well as to interest groups, constituents, and other components of the task environment, leaders generally have the advantage of knowing how members are likely to vote when the voting begins.

Conference committees. It is common knowledge that conference committees are created in order to iron out differences between House and Senate versions of a bill, that the Speaker in the House and the president in the Senate appoint the conferees, and that the chairman of the appropriate standing committee is usually consulted prior to appointments. It is less well understood that the conference committee may be used as a holding device, pending completion of bargaining between the governor and legislative leaders, particularly when they belong to opposite parties, as well as between the two houses of the legislature. By controlling the decisions regarding conferees on bills, the leaders are able to follow through on agreements reached with the governor. This capability would be weakened if conference-committee reports were amenable on the floor of the House and Senate. As it is, the members can only decide whether to accept or reject a conference-committee report.

Given the time constraints, it is probably necessary to the maintenance of the dominant technology that the leaders make the decisions they do and that they enjoy the commensurate powers. However, it may be possible to develop an alternative to the present system that would encompass the bargaining that is so necessary in a bicameral legislature and in a structure in which the governor exercises a veto power.

Gubernatorial vetoes. The Kansas Constitution requires that legislative action be taken, first in the house of origin, to sustain or override a governor's veto of a bill, so that at this final stage in the lawmaking process, no leadership action is necessary. Leaders may facilitate the opportunity to override by preparing the resolution to bring the legislature back into session following adjournment. They may also test the sentiment of each house to determine whether a veto can be overridden by the necessary two-thirds vote, and they may advise the members accordingly; but in general, confrontation action requires very little from the leaders. Party leaders are likely to be more prominent in efforts to sustain or override a veto, since such action is often considered to be important to the party's record.

The Emerging Technology

The fiscal staff. No appointments are as important to the legislative functions of overseeing the operations of the executive branch as are the chairmanships of the Ways and Means committees of both the House and the Senate. The dominant technology can survive several weak standing-committee chairmen, but legislative overseeing fails if the chairmen of both Ways and Means committees lack not only the commitment to this function but also the imagination to see the potential importance that their actions have for state government. Not only are these chairmen the superiors of the fiscal staff, but they also serve on the Post Audit Committee.

The executive budget has long been a more important policy document than the governor's legislative message.[2] Extracting from the budget the policy decisions that are embedded in it is the task of the fiscal staff of the Legislative Research Department. The continued development of this staff depends on its effectiveness in serving the legislature, particularly the members of the Ways and Means committees and ultimately the elected leaders of the legislature. The leaders have the responsibility of communicating the findings and results to the other members of the House and Senate and of placing on the legislature's agenda the appropriate proposals for action. The decisions that they make in this respect are vital to the subdominant technology.

Decisions concerning appropriations determine what services the state government will provide. Scrutiny of budgets, in the sense of legislative overseeing, means evaluation of agency programs and, potentially, recommendations of programs that should be discontinued or strengthened. Limited general-revenue funds in a time of proliferating and increasingly demanding public problems gives special significance to the work of the Ways and Means committees and of the staff that serves these committees.

All standing committees should be, and often are, involved in overseeing the operations of the executive branch. For this reason, the elected leaders must make known to the committee chairmen, whom they appoint, the purposes and techniques of this investigative technology. But in 1976 only the fiscal staff and the postaudit staff are developing techniques of inquiry. Because it is expected that the elected leaders will devote more time to legislative matters than will rank-and-file members, their decisions and nondecisions have the greatest impact on the subdominant technology.

Reviewing the rules and regulations. The elected leaders delegate the review function to special or standing committees. To this initial decision-making responsibility, which is essential if this part of the subdominant technology is to work, should be added the responsibility of reviewing the work of the reviewers, that is, assessing the results of their reviews. If too many policy decisions are made by agencies in the process of developing rules and regulations, it is probably an indication that too many enactments are ambiguous or inadequate in one respect or another. Initiatives for improving them are the responsibility of elected leaders.

Postaudit. The Post Audit Committee is a statutory committee whose members are the elected leaders or their designees and the chairmen of the Ways and Means committees. Their concerns trigger program audits. Such audits are conducted only when the Post Audit Committee decides that they should be undertaken. Not only do the members of this committee share the responsibility for initiating audits, they also share the responsibility for any action or lack of action that follows the completion of each program audit. Agencies may move to correct deficiencies revealed in an audit report, so that further action by the legislature becomes unnecessary. But whatever actions the agencies may take, the follow-up responsibility belongs to the leaders.

No analysis has yet been made of what actions have been taken by the Post Audit Committee and the leaders after receipt of audit reports. That kind of analysis would be an appropriate self-assessment for the leaders of the legislature to perform. It should be coupled with an admonition from the leaders to the members to read the program-audit reports. Few legislators understand the overseeing work of the postaudit staff, largely because they haven't read the reports.

Summary

The effectiveness of the organizations in achieving their goals and objectives depends in part on the skills of leadership. Most technologies do not work or do not work effectively unless leaders make certain kinds of decisions regarding the maintenance and enhancement of technology. In part 1 we have identified the kinds of decisions that elected leaders make in the operation of legislative processes in Kansas. Left unanswered, for the most part, are the questions of how leadership should be structured and what powers the leaders should be permitted to exercise. The omission is not intended to denigrate the importance of these questions, however, because, as the authors of *The Federalist Papers* put it, powers must be commensurate with responsibilities.

The use of the word "powers" also raises questions. Here the word "authority" could be substituted for power. In a broader sense, power is the ability to persuade. Making legislative technologies work effectively requires more than authority to make certain kinds of decisions; it places a heavy demand on leaders' skills of persuasion.

PART 2

Though factional struggles for power may be more characteristic of modern corporations and large public agencies than is generally realized, factionalism is not accepted, rationalized, and institutionalized in these organizations as it is in legislatures. Manipulation of an organization's technologies for factional purposes, particularly in the private sector, would generally be perceived as threatening to the survival of that organization.

In legislatures, leaders are chosen by political parties (factions) or often by factions within the parties. Dependence on these groups for selecting individuals to fill leadership positions makes some role conflict probable if not inevitable. A legislative leader is not free to devote all his energies to technological efficiency, nor is he free to make all decisions on the basis of institutional needs. Though it is possible to achieve role congruence through the exercise of leadership skills under conditions that are not easy to specify, it must be assumed that legislative leaders have to compromise and adjust to the demands of conflicting roles.

Consider, however, the decisions that legislative leaders *could* make if enhancement of technology were the only expectation they needed to satisfy. For committee chairmanships, persons known for their knowledge of subject matter and their ability to preside could be appointed. Bills could be assigned to committees on the basis of no considerations other than functional domain and distribution of the work load. The work of chairmen and committee members could be evaluated by standards of diligence, objectivity, and thoroughness and by the relative absence of ambiguities in the bills that they recommended for passage. The members of committees and committee assignments could be determined solely by reference to the constraints of work loads and time. Staff members could be told to show no favoritism in responding to the requests of members. Priority in hearings could be given to those witnesses who promise to contribute most to the members' needs for information. Bills would be permitted to be considered strictly on their merits; no effort would be made to ensure or prevent passage of bills because of who is sponsoring them. Choices of policy problems to study during the interim could be determined by an environment-scanning system that would identify public problems needing attention.

Yet uncertainties would plague legislative leaders even if they were free from partisan influences. In the absence of such freedom, proposals regarding the maintenance and improvement of technology must be viewed through the perceptual screen of party politics. (The most general effect that this condition has on leaders is that they suffer technology weaknesses to continue if the costs of remedies involve losses in their ability to manipulate decisions for partisan advantage.) Toleration of ineptness is viewed as preferable to violation of political rules such as "Reward your friends, and punish your enemies."

The political constraints that impede or prevent technological changes that are intended to increase efficiency become most evident when buffering proposals are considered. To buffer is to protect the technology from internal and external influences that might impair rationality. Although certain buffering decisions have been made in the Kansas legislature as a result of initiatives on the part of leaders and members, all buffering proposals are likely to be tested on the basis of their probable political and institutional effects.

While partisan considerations tend to conserve existing procedures, institutional role expectations tend to encourage innovations. When leaders seek to define and articulate the mission of the legislature, to defend its integrity and autonomy, and to keep partisanship within the limits that public interests appear to require, then leaders become motivated to improve legislative technologies.[3]

Thinking about the public's expectations and perceptions of the legislature requires looking at the interests of the constituency as a whole. Concern for the legislature's reputation also invites strategies for improvement.

Both former Speaker Duane McGill and House Minority Leader Richard Loux explain their early efforts to improve legislative operations as having stemmed from public criticism of the legislature. Following the 1971 session, Governor Robert Docking gave numerous speeches that were highly critical of legislative actions and inactions. It was Speaker McGill's conclusion that in confrontations with the governor, the legislature had come out second best and that a strategy of strengthening the legislative institution was in order. Representatives McGill and Loux began to collaborate in efforts to increase staff and to enhance the legislature's ability to make policy decisions. Means of overseeing the operations of the executive branch (the emerging technology) were adopted during their tenure.

Sometimes, internal pressures are conducive to changes in technology. The leadership's decision to end the Legislative Council and to substitute for it the system of interim committees governed by a coordinating council—a move that was prompted and supported by former Senate President Glee Smith and Representative Duane McGill—is illustrative of the fact that a legislature's professional reputation is not the only impetus to technology innovation. In this case the demand of rank-and-file legislators (who were excluded from membership on the former Legislative Council) for a role in interim action caused a major change in the agenda-building process.

The definition and articulation of mission, as well as defenses of the legislature's integrity and autonomy, are institutional leadership roles that their offices permit, if not require. Position or office puts leaders in public forums—for example, press conferences and public meetings—where they are obliged to speak for the institution as well as for their party. How they respond to these opportunities is in part a function of personality characteristics.

The more one reflects about leadership roles in a legislature, the more evident it becomes that leaders define the legislative organization's goals as well as manage its technologies. How the leaders individually and collectively perform the task of goal definition depends on their breadth of perspective, that is, on their ability to perceive and balance their several roles.

7
Legislative Staff

The Kansas legislature has not had the resources (the time and expertise) to cope with the myriad tasks and problems that come before it. As a consequence, the legislature has established suborganizations to help accomplish the tasks associated with lawmaking and to assist in making the dominant and emerging technologies work. In this chapter we explore the functions of some of these legislative staff organizations and their relationship to the legislative technologies of lawmaking and overseeing.

Legislative staffs are not a substitute for the functions of legislators, but rather are intended to enable the legislature to enlarge its activities in order to produce desired outcomes.[1]

The evolution of the Kansas legislature as a more independent and complex organization has been marked by the evolution of legislative staff organizations. As the technology of the legislature has changed, so has the support system that is necessary in order to make the technology work.

The Kansas legislature has always had staff to help it accomplish its tasks. The first legislature in 1861 and the preceding territorial legislature were supported by a small staff, which was used primarily to manage the technology (desk staff) and the floors of the two houses (sergeant at arms). One of the principal ways the legislature has used for improving its technology—to increase its searching and learning capabilities in order to make better decisions—has been through the enlargement and addition of staff.

Chapter 9 sketches the evolution of staff in the Kansas legislature and the role that the staff has played in making the legislature a more autonomous, complex, and coherent organization. That discussion of staff, which is a brief investigation of the important functions that legislative staff perform for the legislature, does not adequately reflect the recent changes in three legislative staff organizations that have significantly affected the legislative technology. This chapter is an examination of three staff organizations that perform important functions for the legislature and reflect the changing nature of support staff in the Kansas legislature. The three staff organizations are the Legislative Research Department, the Division of Post Audit, and the Administrative Services Office.

PART 1

The Legislative Research Department

The services of professional, nonpartisan research staff have been available to members and committees of the Kansas legislature since 1934, when the Research Department was created by the Legislative Council. When the Legislative Coordinating Council was established in 1971 to replace the Legislative Council, the Legislative Research Department was continued (but as a statutory agency) under the direction and supervision of the Legislative Coordinating Council.

In terms of staff organization, the seven legislative leaders who compose the council appoint the director of the department (who may be removed by a vote of five of the seven members). The director, in turn, is responsible for the appointment and removal of the other members of the department, all of whom are in the unclassified civil service.

Beginning in 1974, two types of staff professionals have been employed in the department—research analysts and fiscal analysts. Generally speaking, fiscal analysts work primarily with the Ways and Means committees, while research analysts work largely with the other standing and interim committees. However, as circumstances and subject matter dictate, any of the professional staff may be working with any of the committees at a given time.

In a typical fiscal year the department might have authorization for the following staff positions, not all of which are necessarily filled: a director, an associate director, a chief legislative fiscal analyst, four research associates, two principal fiscal analysts, four principal analysts, four research analysts, five fiscal analysts, and seven research assistants, for a total of twenty-nine professional staff positions. The department also has an office manager and is authorized to have eight clerical positions. The major function of the department is to perform research and fiscal services for the legislature, its committees, and individual legislators. The staff members of the department work closely for and with three statutory committees—the Legislative Coordinating Council, the Legislative Budget Committee, and the Legislative Postsecondary Educational Planning Committee (the 1202 Commission).

The department provides staff for all legislative committee meetings that are held both during the session and between sessions. The staff members prepare and distribute timely memoranda and other reports as are appropriate for the committees and, on some occasions, for the legislature as a whole.

During a session, one professional staff member from the department, in addition to a staff attorney from the Revisor of Statutes Office, will be assigned the primary responsibility for a given standing committee, with one other department staff member having backup responsibilities. (Incidentally, the staffs of the Legislative Research Department and the Revisor of Statutes Office work closely on many of their legislative assignments.)

In the past, the exact duties and services provided to a standing committee by the research staff have varied somewhat, depending on the desires of the individual committee chairman. Similarly, the role of the staff or the amount of staff participation in meetings and hearings has varied.

As a rule, however, minimum staff services have included providing assistance in the preparation of agendas for meetings, arranging for participants in meetings and hearings, preparing pertinent informational memoranda, and analyzing and summarizing bills and amendments. Given the time and opportunity to do so, the staff may be called on to brief the committee members on major questions or issues that will come before them in connection with a bill and, at times, to develop policy alternatives for consideration by the members.

During a session, staff members work with individual legislators in developing information that may lead to the drafting of a bill. They may also assist individual members with developing additional background on a bill or an issue, and they represent a resource to aid the members in responding to inquiries or problems of constituents.

Immediately following a session, for the information of the members and other interested persons, the department prepares and publishes a summary of the legislation that was enacted. In the past, many of the members have found this to be a valuable source to use in making talks or in replying to questions after a session has ended.

Interim activities of the staff closely resemble those described for legislative sessions. As prescribed by statute, the staff assists in preparing agendas, sends out notifications of meetings, prepares and presents research information in accordance with committee instructions, and so forth. During the interim, however, departmental staff members are also responsible for preparing minutes of committee meetings and drafts of committee reports and recommendations.

In addition to these assignments, the staff will occasionally prepare research reports for general use and distribution (e.g., *Kansas Tax Facts*). Upon request, the staff also will meet with caucuses of both parties in both houses to explain technical aspects of major legislation. Also, the staff engages in research projects for individual legislative leaders of both parties. Unless staff members are directed to do otherwise, they will treat each legislator's request for research assistance on a confidential basis.

In addition to doing work directly involving legislators and legislative committees, the Legislative Research Department serves as a source of information for federal, state, and local governmental agencies, legislative staff agencies in other states, national organizations and associations, interest groups, and the general public. The staff also works closely with the staffs of executive agencies on such matters as revenue-estimating and school finance.

Because the Revisor of Statutes Office, the Legislative Reference Library, and the Division of Legislative Post Audit are in a better position to answer certain types of inquiries than is the Legislative Research Department, these offices work closely together and will transfer questions from one office to another when it seems appropriate to do so.

The major technological question that arises in preparing materials on major policy issues is that of the form and content of such briefings. In the past, the Research Department analysts have tried to provide the information that committee chairmen and legislative leaders have requested. As a consequence, generally speaking, staff materials have not been prepared in a form that would structure committee deliberations, by identifying alternatives and projecting the consequences of alternatives.

In summary, the Research Department has changed considerably since it was established in 1934. The most significant changes have been in three areas. Beginning in 1934 and immediately thereafter, the Research Department functioned primarily as the research arm of the Legislative Council. Its duties involved researching problems assigned by the council and providing reports with conclusions and, at times, specific recommendations of the council committees for legislation. The Research Department changed as the Legislative Council evolved into the Coordinating Council, as the legislature began to meet every year, and as its committees began to meet more frequently during the interim. As a result of these changes, the Research Department became less the research arm of the council and more a general research resource for the standing committees and the general membership. The more general and long-range research has given way to immediate research questions required by committees.

Because of the increasing demand on the part of the legislature for committee assistance, the Research Department has become more specialized. The Research Department now staffs the standing committees of both houses with professional personnel who have backgrounds in agriculture, education, health, and other policy areas. Thus, the staff of the Research Department has become more specialized in policy areas and less oriented to generalists whose research interests cross committee jurisdictions.

The orientation of the Research Department has changed because of a significant enlargement of its scope. In addition to its primary work as the policy research resource for the legislature, the department has added a fiscal staff which has the responsibilities previously described.

The Legislative Post Audit Division

It will be noted in chapter 9 that until 1971 the postaudit functions for the legislature were carried out through the elected state auditor.

According to one observer, "[The State Auditor] was an entity in himself, not in the Legislative or Executive Branches of government. He did a financial audit only and his staff were not trained professionals and often learned their work from more or less on-the-job experience."[2]

After the legislature had established its own Post Audit Division, the tradition of financial auditing continued. As a result of the appointment of the new legislative postauditor and because of increasing pressure from the legislature for more extensive audits, the division began to augment its staff and to conduct audits of program performance. The 1976 annual report of the Legislative Division of Post Audit describes the difference between the traditional financial audits and performance audits:

> Legislative Post Audit provides the legislature with information necessary to evaluate the work of governmental agencies. Today, as legislators and administrators try increasingly to allocate tax dollars effectively and make government work more efficiently, that information becomes even more important. As a result, Legislative Post Audit has broadened the scope of its audits.
>
> Traditionally, an audit of a governmental agency has been thought of as a *financial audit*, that is, as an accountant's examination of an agency's financial records and procedures to determine whether the agency's financial operations are sound and in accordance with state law. Part of Legislative Post Audit's work is directed toward an examination of each state agency's financial operations at least once every two years.
>
> Increasingly, however, legislators and citizens want to know more about an agency's performance. Often it is not enough to know whether an agency is spending its appropriation in accordance with state law. Other questions arise: Are the programs of an agency accomplishing what they were set up to do? Are the programs run as efficiently as possible? Do they provide any real benefit to the citizens of the State?
>
> Such questions are answered in a *performance audit*, an audit that examines an agency, a program, or a group of programs to assess efficiency and effectiveness. Such audits may have several parts. Because precise details of programs are not always spelled out in legislation, performance auditors must examine available evidence to determine the program's intended goals. Performance auditors must also examine agency intent. Important differences between legislative and agency intent may surface during this part of a performance audit.
>
> A performance audit may also measure how well a program's objectives are being met (program results auditing or effectiveness audit-

ing). It can also measure how efficiently the program is conducted (operational auditing). To make such evaluations, performance auditors use a variety of techniques and research methods from business, management, and the social sciences.[3]

In 1974 the legislature appointed a new legislative postauditor, who had a more diverse training in auditing and accounting, which reflected, in his words, a change in the orientation of most accountants: "We question the efficiency and effectiveness—the impact—of programs based solely on a financial audit. A financial audit does not address all of the components of a program."[4] Until 1974 most of the staff for the Post Audit Division were oriented toward financial audits; and for the most part, they were students working part time. Since 1974 the staff has consisted of full-time professionals, trained in accounting, business, public administration, law, and other related fields. The level of expertise and the variety of backgrounds in the staff have enabled Legislative Post Audit to develop the ability to perform program audits and high-quality audits of the financial affairs and transactions of state agencies.[5] The budget that the legislature appropriated for the Post Audit Division reflects this substantial change, as do the levels of expenditure reported in table 7.1

The extension of the legislature's responsibility for the administration and implementation of a policy of legislative overseeing has required a substantial change in the orientation of the postaudit staff

TABLE 7.1
BUDGET OF THE DIVISION OF POST AUDIT

Year	Amount
(Auditor)	
1954	$ 88,035
1955	102,248
1960	112,199
1961	117,171
1970	163,020
1971	169,230
(Division of Legislative Post Audit)	
1974	489,470
1975	580,511
1976 (estimate)	864,689

SOURCE: State of Kansas Annual Budgets.

of the Kansas legislature. The extension of the overseeing function has also required a substantial increase in personnel and expertise in order to accomplish the more complicated task of financial- and program-auditing.

Legislative Administrative Services

In every complex organization there are organized activities that are supportive of the technology. They are specialized and instrumental to the maintenance of those activities directly related to the purposes for which the organization exists. These "housekeeping" services include such essential work as personnel recruitment, payroll, security, and building maintenance. Though vital to the operation of the legislative technology, support activities are separate because they require special skills and knowledge and because they can be organized in various ways and yet remain supportive of the legislature's primary task of lawmaking. Their goals and objectives can be formulated, and their activities can be organized, somewhat independently of what happens in the operation of the legislative technology. The degree of independence depends on how crucial the support activity is to the operation of the legislature.

But what are these administrative services that must be performed? Who is responsible for the preparation of schedules for the use of committee rooms; the planning of office assignments; the recruitment and instruction of secretaries and file clerks during the session; the keeping of records regarding payroll, expenses, health insurance, and retirement; the operation of the documents room and supervision of pages; and a number of other associated tasks? The answer to all these questions is the director and staff of the Division of Legislative Administrative Services. "Housekeeping" is a label that is sometimes used to describe these activities, but it is inadequate to the range of tasks encompassed under the "administrative services" umbrella. The sensitivities of people in matters of personal comfort and convenience (parking, for example) prevent these tasks from becoming routine, and they require the evolution of support staff to assure that services are available (means instrumental to the attainment of ends).

Aspects of most of the service activities affect the dominant technology in ways suggested below.

Allocation of space. To process all bills in a period of ninety days or less and to ensure careful consideration of those that are most important to public well-being is a formidable task, even when facilities are adequate. It becomes an impossible task when committees are limited to a daily session of one hour. That limitation arises from the fact that there are only twelve committee rooms to accommodate nineteen House and fifteen Senate committees. Only the House and Senate Ways and Means committees are assigned rooms that are always available for their meetings, an advantage that is necessitated by the work loads of these two committees.

The space problem affects the lawmaking process in another way. Although many people are interested in attending committee hearings, each of the two rooms that can be used for them accommodates less than a hundred spectators. So the right of constituents and representatives of interest groups to watch and hear and testify is attenuated by the space problem. While crowds are not knocking on committee doors, demanding entry every day, congestion is typical enough to concern legislators who are committed to the principle of easy access of citizens to policy-making arenas.

The availability of adequate office space is a less serious problem in the state capitol. Representatives and senators can use their desks in the chambers to answer mail and make telephone calls, to read bills, and to perform other duties. Though offices are a convenience or, for some, a necessity, the problem of office space less seriously affects lawmaking than does the shortage of space for committee meetings.

Today, senators and representatives both share office suites, though senators are privileged to have private cubicles in their suites. Committee chairmen occupy offices that are fashioned out of air shafts, which, given space conditions, could be considered luxurious accommodations.

The space problems described above indicate one of the constraints that limit the ability of Administrative Services to provide adequate facilities for lawmaking, for overseeing the operations of the executive branch and supportive activities.

Recruitment and supervision of staff. Approximately forty secretaries and file clerks are employed during every session. Each senator is permitted to hire a secretary of his own choosing; representatives share secretarial services. The number of applicants is more than the number of jobs available, but the number who are capable of taking shorthand is usually fewer than desired. Hence, those who have ad-

vanced skills are usually assigned to committee chairpersons and
serve as both committee and office secretaries.

Only the positions of secretary of the Senate, chief clerk of the
House, sergeants at arms, and doorkeepers are appointed by the
Speaker in the House and the president in the Senate. Although party
affiliation is a condition of employment for these positions, it is not
a qualification for most clerical positions.

Pages, who are of junior- or senior-high-school age, are not considered staff, though two supervisors of pages are employees in the
Office of Administrative Services. Every senator and representative is
allocated a certain number of pages per session. During a single session, more than twenty-seven hundred young Kansans experience a
day's work in the Kansas legislature.

Documents and printing. Each morning of a session the Documents Room dispenses bills, journals, calendars, subject indexes, bill
supplements, and status reports on bills—all printed during the night
by the State Printing Office. Personnel in the Administrative Services
Division have the task collecting and transporting to the printing
office all of the documents required the following morning. During
the interim, the office is responsible for printing numerous other
documents.

Though it is periodically proposed that the state get out of the
printing business, it is difficult to see how the legislature's printing
needs could be served without a state-owned printing plant.

Parking. By law, 140 parking spaces around the Statehouse are
reserved for legislators. This number is more than what is needed
during the interim but less than what is needed during a session. It is
a perplexing problem for the Division of Administrative Services.
Like most Americans everywhere, everyone who works in the Statehouse wants to be guaranteed parking space within a few steps of
the building.

Payroll, insurance, and retirement. In Kansas in 1976, legislators received thirty-five dollars per calendar day, plus an expense
allowance not to exceed forty-four dollars per day. In addition, each
legislator was entitled to thirteen cents per mile for one round trip
per week from his home to the capitol. The payroll and voucher requi-
sitions and records are the responsibility of Administrative Services.
In addition, this office maintains health insurance and retirement systems, each equivalent to what is available to state employees generally.

Post office and supplies. Processing the volume of incoming and outgoing mail is essentially the responsibility of the United States Post Office, but Administrative Services maintains a metering machine and records the flow of mail. Each legislator is allowed to mail out no more than twenty-five letters per day.

Supplies are requisitioned for legislators from those available to all state agencies under purchasing contracts. Administrative Services provides legislators and legislative staff with supplies as needed. A minor grievance is the occasional demand for supplies that are not available through purchase contracts.

Notices. The Division of Administrative Services is an important link in the legislature's communications system. The office mails out notices of committee meetings (including agenda) to more than a thousand citizens and organizations. This service is provided without charge and on request. In addition, letters from legislative leaders to members and a variety of other communications are transmitted by the office.

Although the "housekeeping" services of the Kansas legislature may appear to be an insignificant part of the legislature's tasks, the recognition of the importance of these support activities can be seen in the legislature's creation of a special office—Administrative Services —to better control and coordinate these various support activities that have become increasingly vital to the operation of the legislature. The Office of Administrative Services is a reflection of the growing complexity of the legislature itself.

PART 2

Legislative Information Requirements

Information is the currency of legislative transactions. Appraisal is the essence of the process by which information is converted into decisions. In practice, the collecting and dispensing of information is not neatly treated as a specialized activity distinct from that of appraisal or evaluation of it, but these are analytically separable functions. By thinking of intelligence (information-gathering) and appraisal as distinguishable activities, the differences in the roles of the three staff organizations come into focus. The Legislative Research Department is an intelligence operation. The Division of Legislative

Post Audit is primarily an appraisal instrument. Legislative Administrative Services performs the tasks of recording and transmitting information.

Legislators request and receive information and appraisals, and they devote most of their energies to evaluating appraisals and to utilizing information in the making of policy decisions. The questions they ask of the Legislative Research Department, as well as the questions they do *not* ask, reveal the intelligence-gathering and appraising roles both of legislators and of research staff.

In general, legislators request information that is relevant to any or all of the following questions:

1. What is the nature of the problem to which a given bill is addressed (or, in the case of an interim study committee, what is the nature of the problem that has been assigned to the committee)?

2. What are the facts with respect to a specific aspect of the bill or problem?

3. How have other states addressed the problem?

4. What would be the fiscal, organizational, and social effects of a bill or proposal if enacted?

In general, legislators do *not* ask the research staff to provide answers to the following kinds of questions:

1. What interest groups will like or not like the bill or proposal?

2. Will my chances for reelection be enhanced or diminished by enactment of a bill?

3. How will other legislators (and the party leadership or caucus) read the effects of the bill or proposal?

4. What long-range impacts would enactment of the proposal be likely to have on the environment or the system?

In a separate category is the question "What problems of implementation are likely if a bill or proposal were to be enacted?" This question may or may not be asked. If it is, it is likely to be phrased in specific terms.

The first three questions that are not generally asked are political and, as such, belong to the domain in which the legislators consider themselves either to be knowledgeable or to have outside sources of information. They also depend on lobbyists and hearings to provide information about the attitudes, beliefs, and strategies of interest groups. There is no methodological reason that the research staff could not obtain answers to political questions, but there are other considerations that tend to place such questions outside the domain of the research staff. One is that legislators prefer to interact directly with representatives of interest groups rather than through intermediaries. Another is that they believe it is desirable to buffer the research staff's technology from the influence of interest groups. Still another is that legislators don't want any member of the staff to make surveys of the attitudes of other legislators unless that staff member is a personally selected aide. Such surveys would affect strategies in ways that might limit the legislators' options.

The last question (about long-range impacts) is not generally asked, because legislators are not programed to think about issues in this way. The incremental nature of legislative policy-making, skepticism about the reliability of long-range projections, and a preoccupation with political effects are also parts of the explanation.

It seems evident that the intelligence-gathering role of the Legislative Research Department can be expanded to include more information about (1) possible problems of implementation and (2) long-range and systemic impacts of policy proposals. But it is equally evident that such role expansion will not occur automatically. The reasons lie in such characteristics of organizations like the Kansas legislature as:

1. The shortness of the sessions and the large number of bills to be processed preclude in-depth consideration of any bill More intelligence would simply compound the logistical problem.

2. Citizen legislators, unlike full-time, professional legislators, have little opportunity or incentive to become "professional" in their approach to policy issues.

3. The work load of a relatively small central research staff discourages efforts to expand intelligence-gathering activities.

4. The norm of "responsiveness" inhibits staff initiatives toward expansion (the staff risks criticism from legislators for providing more than what is expected and requested).

5. The lack of an organized and sophisticated socialization process for legislators means that demands for more and in-depth intelligence will remain entirely a function of who is elected.

The prospects for a marked expansion of the intelligence-gathering role of the Legislative Research staff in Kansas are not bright. If and when expansion occurs, it will probably be a consequence of the election of leaders who are able and willing to devote most of their time and energies to the legislature.

The conditions that affect performance of the Legislative Research Department have less impact on the staff of the Legislature's Post Audit Division, because performance evaluation (appraisal) is less dependent upon what legislators ask and demand. The staff of the Division of Post Audit is relatively uninvolved in the operation of the dominant technology. The work of individual staff members is assigned by the administrators of the division rather than by committee chairmen and other legislators. But in the end, the policy-making effects of what the Division of Post Audit produces may be limited by the same organizational characteristics that constrain expansion of the Research Department. Performance audits are only effective tools for agenda-building and overseeing if the legislators are disposed to employ them to those purposes. Time will tell.

8
Networks of Communication and Socialization

Just as some elements of the primary technologies are, upon closer examination, more than mere routine, such as the bill-drafting phase of the dominant technology, some aspects of the supportive technologies of communications networks and socialization processes are, from the perspective of organizational theory, more than mere routine. Like the circulatory system in the human organism, the internal networks of communication branch outward to link the various components of the legislative organization and to assist in the process of coordinating those components whose collective efforts are necessary to the effective operation of the legislative process. In addition, the web of communications extends outward to embrace elements of the task environment and, beyond that, to establish linkages with the outer environment. The legislative process is similarly aided by the processes of socialization that work to establish a framework of common values and acceptable norms of behavior with which members are encouraged to comply.

PART 1

Communications in the Dominant Technology

Amitai Etzioni makes a distinction between instrumental and expressive communications.[1] The distinction is a useful one, because it separates the communications that are readily exposed to public view (such as floor debate or the submission of testimony before a committee) from the complex administrative and technical communications that permeate the process and give it life. For Etzioni, the former are *expressive*; the latter, *instrumental*. His taxonomy of communications systems, however, can be subjected to further refinements in order to identify more specific types of communications in the legislature, especially those of an instrumental nature.

It will serve, at this point, to enumerate what varieties of communication exist in the legislature, and it will remain to demonstrate how and to what extent those communications processes lend support to the effective operation of the primary technologies. Expressive communications generally include verbal expressions by legislators in support of or in opposition to passage of legislation during debate before the Committee of the Whole or in the course of considering legislation or hearing testimony in any of the standing committees. In contrast, instrumental communications are more frequently nonverbal. Many kinds of communicative devices are, in fact, unknown outside the organization. They include the technical instrument, which always takes a written form; the nontechnical instrument, which may be verbal or nonverbal; and nontechnical information, which analyzes policy considerations in order to facilitate decision-making or which records information generated by legislative action.

The communications networks that operate in the dominant technology have several dimensions. The leadership most frequently directs its messages downward and outward, either to members of the entire organization or to party members. Vertical communications in an upward direction occur when a subunit reports to a component of the organization or to the organization itself—for example, when a subcommittee reports to the full committee or when a standing committee reports to the Committee of the Whole. Communications with staff may be viewed as horizontal, insofar as the legislative process is conceived as a sequential process within and between two houses of equal authority, with a complex network of communications between staff and legislators all along the arduous path to passage.

Interorganizational Communications

Communications in the dominant technology begin in the environment and take several forms. Expressions of opinion and self-interest are presented directly to special committees during the interim and to individual legislators by letter, phone, or word of mouth. In addition, such expressions are indirectly communicated to legislative decision-makers who are perceptive to events transpiring in the environment; thus legislators may buffer the impact of direct pressures from lobbyists or interest groups by making themselves aware of those occurrences and pronouncements. The special interim committee, in turn, submits a report, with the assistance of the Legislative Research Department and the Revisor of Statutes Office, which contains background information on the approved study proposals, the committee's recommendations, and proposed legislation to implement the recommendations. The annual report on interim studies, therefore, represents several forms of communication: an expression of the committee's conclusions and suggestions for change; information to facilitate policy-making; and technical instruments—that is, proposed legislation.

Another form of communication originating outside the legislative organization, but within the task environment, is the *Governor's Legislative Message*. It likewise represents a form of expressive communications, providing a summarization of those issues which the governor believes merit consideration (and approval) by the legislature.

Most communications between the environment and the legislative organization tend to flow in the direction of the latter, much in the manner of David Easton's organizational demands and supports in systems theory. But also contained in that model is a feedback mechanism which relates outputs to subsequent inputs. Media communications in the form of news articles, editorials, and public-service broadcasts provide that vital link between the environment and the legislative organization. In establishing that linkage continuously throughout the legislative process, media communications serve to keep legislators informed of public reaction to their decisions and simultaneously to keep the public informed of legislative events as they occur.

The media occupy a rather unique position in the communications system of the legislature inasmuch as they do not form either a part of the legislative organization itself or a part of the task environment. Since their purpose is to provide information of interest to their patrons, they must be selective in the information that they communicate. The selective process may result in some distortion or omission of facts that some observers and participants believe to be important. But virtually all legislators seek to establish favorable relations with members of the media, as evidenced by the media's privilege of having access to the floor of either chamber when the legislature is convened.

Intraorganizational Communications

Technical communications. The bill-drafting phase of the dominant technology, which primarily engages the professional services of the Revisor of Statutes Office, involves the transformation of the concepts and concerns embodied in the various forms of expressive communications into a communicative instrument that, when duly approved, possesses the full force and effect of law. This attribute of form of proper legal language, together with the fact that it must be formally adopted, is what characterizes a technical communicative instrument. A bill, therefore, qualifies as one type of technical instrument. Indeed, inasmuch as the passage of legislation is the primary function in the dominant technology, a bill is the quintessential technical instrument, communicating legislative intent, along with the authorizing and directive content, to those who will implement the law.

Because the Revisor of Statutes Office, among legislative staff agencies, is responsible for preparing all technical communicative instruments, the communicative relationship between the Revisor of Statutes Office and the legislative product is essentially a network that runs parallel to the path of legislation as it passes through the legislative process. An amendment, for example, may be offered for consideration at several points in the process—during committee action, floor action, or in conference committee. The revisor in most instances prepares the amendments, including the translation into proper legal form of those amendments which are approved "conceptually." The significance of the amendment as an example of instrumental communications lies in the fact that it possesses the capability of modifying the language of a bill as it was originally introduced. Its importance is further emphasized by contrasting it with the nontechnical nature of an expressive communication, which, without being translated into the technical language of the system, has no material impact on the final form of the bill. For example, it is not uncommon for one or more legislators, in the course of discussion on a bill, to voice an objection without having prepared an amendment in advance as a vehicle with which to effect a change that would overcome that objection. If the discussion arises in committee, the legislator who is objecting may offer a "conceptual" amendment; however, if the matter has surfaced during floor debate, the legislator is often compelled to delay final action or to seek to have the bill referred again to committee for further consideration.

Another technical instrument of communication is the committee report. It, too, must assume a legal form, since it embodies amendments, made by the committee, that must be formally adopted by the Committee of the Whole.

The Revisor of Statutes Office, therefore, serves as a translator of nontechnical communications into the technical—that is, legal—language of the system, which at the same time constitutes a separate and identifiable communications network extending continuously the entire length of the lawmaking process, from the genesis of a bill to its enrollment. Inasmuch as the product of the dominant technology must ultimately take a legal form in order to have the effect of law, the necessity of the translating function to the operation of the organization becomes evident.

Informational communications. Other communications between legislators and staff in the dominant technology involve primarily the Legislative Research Department, whose role in the organization requires it to be proficient in the use of a variety of communicative devices. It should also be noted that although research staff is assigned to specific standing committees, the network of communications involving research staff can be found throughout the legislative process. Essentially, the communications employed are nontechnical instrumental and nontechnical informational.

Probably the most obvious communications between research staff and members of the legislature are informational. In addition to the interim reports already mentioned, which are submitted to the legislature prior to the commencement of each legislative session, information is provided to individual legislators or to members of a committee on request. Information supplied to a committee most often takes the form of an interdepartmental memorandum, whereas information to an individual legislator is conveyed formally via a special form called the "green sheet." The information communicated in response to the legislative request is designed to facilitate the making of policy decisions and may or may not be linked to a particular stage of the dominant technology.

In traditional fashion, information is also communicated verbally by the staff during work with a subcommittee or during a staff briefing before the full committee on such matters as the explanation of a bill or responding to a committee request for information. If, for example, the explanation of a bill concerns the technical language of the bill, the Revisor of Statutes' staff would be in a better position to provide information.

Another variety of informational communications is one that is generated as a result of action taken on legislation (or the effects of such action). These communications serve a dual purpose. First, they represent a summary of action taken to a given point, and second, they serve as information to others at a later stage in the legislative process. As a consequence, these forms of communication are linked closely with the stages of the dominant technology.

One communicative network of this sort is the bill-locater system operated by the Legislative Reference Library and the Revisor of Statutes Office, which tracks the progress of bills through the legislative process. Since 1976 the system has been computerized, with terminals located in key offices throughout the Statehouse, including both the House and Senate chambers. Information concerning floor action in either house may be brought forth almost instantly. In addition, a printed version entitled *Legislative Information Index and Actions Report* is generated from the system and is distributed once a week. The system is therefore conceived as a continuous record of legislative actions pertaining to the passage of legislation, and it parallels the operative stages of the dominant technology.

Another similar system is one that records the fiscal impact of legislation. This system, which started to operate in 1975, is maintained by the legislative fiscal staff. The process begins in the executive branch of government, specifically in the Budget Division, which is required by statute to determine the fiscal impact of all legislation within seven days after a bill is introduced. Legislative fiscal staff makes further adjustments from that point on only as legislation is amended. Beginning with the 1977 legislative session, this system was also computerized, utilizing the House and Senate journals to record amendments. Unlike that of the bill-locater system, the report generated from the system of fiscal-impact information has a limited distribution, primarily to the leadership of both houses and to the Revisor of Statutes Office.

Another form by which information is communicated is supplemental information on bills, commonly referred to as "bill briefs."

These are summaries, written by the Legislative Research Department, of the content of each bill that passes out of committee with a favorable recommendation. Most bill briefs also include background information about what group, individual, or committee recommended the bill for introduction. Bill briefs represent both types of information described previously in this chapter. The summary of a bill's contents is intended to be a condensation of material to make the information contained therein readily accessible; but since it also includes an explanation of any amendments made in committee or on the floor of either house, a bill brief is to that extent a record of action taken during one stage in the legislative process. Moreover, it serves the purpose of translating those contents from the technical language of the bill to nontechnical information, thus providing a link between technical and nontechnical communications networks and thereby performing the reverse translating function from that of the Revisor of Statutes Office.

Nontechnical communications. In contrast to informational systems, nontechnical instrumental communications operate on a lower plane of visibility but constitute, nonetheless, an integral part of the communications network of the legislative process. Instrumental communications of a nontechnical nature have as their most significant attribute the fact that they must further in some way, directly or indirectly, the performance of a specific step in the lawmaking process and need not take a legal form. Some must be formally adopted by members of a committee or a Committee of the Whole. What appears to be a routine or commonplace communication is in fact an indispensable part of the system. An example of a verbal, nontechnical communications instrument would be a motion offered by a committee member which, if adopted, would result in a specific committee action. An elaborate set of "parliamentary" rules, some of which are common to all organizational meetings (such as *Robert's Rules of Order*) and some of which are peculiar to the legislature, has been established to ensure that an orderly procedure among numerous participants will prevail. The motion, if adopted, in any case ultimately assumes a written form. In committee, it is incorporated into the minutes of the meeting, which are themselves adopted; and in the Committee of the Whole, it is included in the journal.

An example of a nontechnical communicative instrument that originates in a written form would be a subcommittee report. It may provide information, just as it may express the subcommittee's intention on a given matter, but it constitutes an instrument because it must be adopted by the full committee. As a communication to the full committee, the directional flow of the communication can be viewed as vertical and upward.

Also operating in the legislative organization are a variety of other communicative devices of a nontechnical nature; they constitute a rather complex network, which, in addition to operating internally in both houses, establishes a link between the two chambers and between either chamber and elements of the task environment, such as the governor or the secretary of state. These communications are for the most part directed and coordinated by the chief clerk in the House and the secretary of the Senate, and they do not require formal adoption in order to serve their purpose. Nevertheless, these communicative instruments are essential to the functioning of the organization, rendering orderly and manageable what appears to the casual observer to be a chaotic "buzz" of activity.

Within the lawmaking processes of each chamber the chief clerk and the secretary receive instructions from the leadership as to the order of business for each legislative day; they also accept and duly record committee reports from committee chairmen concerning bills acted upon in their committees. They also communicate with each other on behalf of their respective chambers to inform the other that a bill has been passed or to communicate concurrences or nonconcurrences when the house of origin accepts or rejects the amendments to a bill that were made by the second house. The form of the bill is altered (enrolled) in preparation for its submission to the governor; and the governor, in vetoing a measure, informs the legislature of his disapproval by a veto message. Mention of this network of communication cannot, of course, be comprehensive but is intended to demonstrate the complexity and multidimensional nature of this formal but largely invisible form of communication.

The House and Senate journals, whose composition is also the responsibility of the chief clerk of the House and the secretary of the Senate, are other examples of nontechnical informational communications, because they contain information generated as a result of actions taken in the lawmaking process and represent an accounting of all the communicative instruments mentioned above. A copy of the journals is sent to the secretary of state, to be maintained there on permanent file.

Expressive communications. Expressive communications within the legislative organization, which include for the most part verbal communications between legislators, are most in evidence during committee action and floor debate. Probably because of the high degree of visibility of these stages of the legislative process, communications in these phases have received more attention than the other types. The visibility of committee action stems from the fact that the organization permits access by elements of the task environment at that point in the decision-making process. However, by the time that policy issues have reached floor debate, the organization buffers its procedures, including communications, by restricting the participation to members. And the act of buffering the environment should not be construed as the result of any political scheming. Rather, it is a feature that is characteristic of many organizations; its purpose is to forbid the uninitiated to participate in its ceremonial processes and to relegate them to the periphery of activity as mere observers or spectators.

Expressive communications, more than any other type, are subject to distortion and dysfunctions in the sense that they sometimes conceal more than they reveal or, in any case, do not facilitate a clear understanding of an issue that is under consideration. An example would be the level of rationalism that prevails in the course of debate. Given the diversity and size of the membership in the legislative organization, communications are necessarily complex. To compensate for the difficulty requires an appeal to some common denominator that is designated to gain wide acceptance—that is, to secure a majority of votes for the purpose of determining the outcomes of decisions. Communicated information about a proposal, then, must be simple enough to be understood and general enough so that each voter may discover some aspect that he or she deems worthy of support. In a symbolic sense, support for that common denominator is likewise justified in general terms, especially as to the benefits that allegedly will accrue to the general populace as a result of the passage of that particular proposal. Therefore, the language of democratic ideology, with its emphasis on seeking benefits for the largest number possible, is easily invoked in order to generate support for a given measure.

In practice, however, the problems confronting decision-makers are not always so easily understood, nor are solutions necessarily so simple and general. The legal language in which bills and amendments are written is, after all, quite specific and technical. The implication for communications is that the verbal forms they assume during committee or floor debate, couched as they are in the generalities and polemics of democratic ideology, are not always conducive to the complex deliberations that actually characterize legislative matters. Not all legislators are attorneys; therefore, debate itself, because of the nature of communications in the organization, is restricted in the degree to which it facilitates decision-making of a technical nature. When a legislator offers an amendment (usually prepared in advance), the reading of the amendment is frequently waived for this very reason, and it is left to the author of the amendment to explain its contents in nontechnical terms. Other legislators, not privileged to have read and studied the amendment in advance, are obliged to accept the explanation presented by its author. To compensate for the deficiency in personal knowledge about a proposal, substitute methods are devised. These might include consideration of the proposal's author; on which side of the aisle that author sits; taking cues from reliable friends (or opponents); and so forth. An informal network of communications is necessary in order to make the cue-taking system work. On any given issue, a number of influential members may be communicating with potential supporters. The communicative linkages may follow partisan lines or various other factional lines, but the pattern created by this communications network may be described as "polynucleated," because each system operates somewhat independently and because the communicative signals flow outward from influential individuals. They cannot, of course, operate with total independence, because many individuals hold membership in more than one faction; thus the elements of this communications network overlap.

At least two potentially dysfunctional elements are at work. The first is the disparity between the nontechnical nature of expressive communications and the technical language of a bill, as it is amended during debate; also there is the problem that arises in translating a position of advocacy in the former into a formally adopted directive in the latter. As previously observed, staff assists the legislature in this translation process, but the assistance does not generally extend into the process of debate. The second element is the ideological language that characterizes debate. The legislator who, in advocating passage of a bill, conceals the beneficial effects to his local district by couching his remarks in democratic ideological language, which emphasizes statewide benefits, is to that extent distorting the content of the communications process.

If the nature of communications in the screening and testing phases of the dominant technology presents a hindrance to the deliberation of technical matters, it also serves as a tool for the obstructionists and the opponents of any given issue. Many an opponent has exploited the situation by imputing a controversial interpretation to some portion of a bill, finding fault with its language, or by deliberately obfuscating it, thus seeking to postpone consideration of the measure. In so doing, communications processes are manipulated to affect decisions without an affirmative commitment to any position by an opponent and without any discussion of the proposal on its merits.

In one sense, communications are essentially negative, given the manner in which they operate. Given a situation in which a tenuous, ephemeral majority determines policy outcomes, it often appears that it is of greater significance to the passage of a bill to avoid offending some than it is to make positive efforts to seek the support of others by a direct appeal to them. For example, many bills are treated routinely and do not stir opposition precisely because no one possesses adequate knowledge of them to generate any effective opposition. Explanations of bills that are presented with some degree of specificity are more likely to be opposed than those in which a cursory statement of the bill's intent is considered to be sufficient. It occurs because the longer the explanation, the greater the probability that it will reveal some aspect of the legislation with which a legislator will disagree.

Leadership

Communications of another dimension are to be found in those between the leadership and others in the legislative organization. They are, for the most part, vertical and downward, though the depth of the vertical dimension is not deep since the hierarchy in the legislative organization is one of only modest proportions. The form of communicative messages coincides with functions performed by the leadership—namely, administrative and partisan.

The Speaker of the House and the majority leader of the Senate have the authority to decide the order of business on each legislative day, the most significant part of which is the order of bills to be considered on general orders. The order of business is communicated each day through the calendars of the respective houses, along with a report on the status of all bills that have been introduced and the committees to which those that have not been reported have been assigned. The Senate calendar also includes the tentative agendas of

Senate committees that will be meeting during the week. The calendars of both houses are distributed daily through the documents room, which is the repository in the Statehouse of all bills, journals, bill briefs, and other legislative documents.

In addition to this instrument of information, leaders are occasionally called upon to submit to questioning by the media, or the leaders may initiate such press conferences themselves in order to present their views on an urgent matter or to explain the progress that the legislature has made to that point in the session. Late in the session, when the institutional differences between the legislature and governor over major issues of policy begin to surface, the legislative leadership is obliged to defend its efforts and accomplishments from gubernatorial criticism. The communications that arise from those circumstances, therefore, are often intended to convey this sort of message to those in the task environment and in the environment at large.

But the leadership represents partisan interests as well as institutional ones. Unlike communications that facilitate the management role of the leadership, intraparty communications are relatively less visible. In view of the importance of the communications system in the legislature, the leaders of both houses seek to maintain some measure of control over the outcome of legislation that is in committees. In order to accomplish this, a close, informally structured network of communications is maintained between leaders and committee chairmen. Committee chairmen must be informed of the legislation that is important to the realization of party goals, and leaders must be kept informed of the status of such legislation in committee.

Committee chairmen may be responsible for gauging the strength of support for legislation in committees, but the leadership assumes that function when legislation reaches the floor. Yet another communications network is essential to accomplish this purpose, and it entails a periodic check for support of a bill among the members. The information thus acquired is necessary to the strategy of leadership in determining when to schedule a bill for debate in order to enhance its chances for passage.

Other strategies among members of both parties have traditionally been plotted in caucus. Prior to the 1976 session, participation in the caucus was confined to party members, and the caucus as a device for communicating strategy, being direct and of close proximity, served the purpose well. But with the advent of "open" caucuses, the argument was made by some that the content of communications would change as a consequence and that really meaningful communications would revert to their former invisible form and would no longer be exposed to public view. Whatever purpose the caucus now serves, the leadership continues to use it as a means for communicating with party members.

PART 2

Variation of Communication

To the extent that processes in the emerging and dominant technologies coincide, networks of communication in each are essentially the same. Reviewing agency budgets, which ultimately entails the passage of appropriations bills, is an integral part of the lawmaking process; so, too, is the approval of agency regulations by the legislature. Postaudit review of agency records, on the other hand, makes the stages of the dominant technology accessible at several key points, particularly the agenda-building phase. Since the function of the emerging technology is the overseeing of agency activities in the executive branch of government, communications between state agencies and the legislature have developed to facilitate the process. In addition, legislative staff must be considered a key point in the communications systems.

Interorganizational Communications

Budget review. Communications in the review of agency budgets generally follow the sequential nature of the budgetary process, which begins in each agency when it submits its budget for the coming fiscal year to the Budget Division. Each state agency is also required by statute to submit a copy of its budget request to the Legislative Research Department by October 1 of each year for legislative review. The budgetary process continues through the budget hearings and, of course, the submission of the governor's recommendations to the legislature. But fiscal staff can begin to examine the budgets of individual agencies prior to the commencement of the legislative session and, therefore, in advance of the governor's recommendations. In addition to this formal, statutory-based flow of communications, which parallels the budget process, a more informal channel has developed between individual agencies and the legislative fiscal staff.

The development of this communicative link arises from the fact that the documents submitted—whether an agency's budget request or the *Governor's Budget Report*—do not in themselves provide all the information that is necessary in order to make an adequate review of executive activities and programs. As a result, fiscal staff is obliged to make contacts with agency representatives to request information, conduct interviews, and arrange visits to state institutions and facilities.

From a purely communications viewpoint, the direct link to the legislature through legislative fiscal staff is designed to clear a path to the source of information so as to reduce the number of intermediate points through which communications must pass. To the extent that the fiscal staff or legislative committees or subcommittees can examine agency activities firsthand, the communications process is simplified, and distortions are reduced. But in most cases, this sort of firsthand information-gathering is not possible. In large measure, then, the role of the fiscal staff is to distill the information it receives from agencies, the Budget Division, and the governor, among others, both qualitatively and quantitatively. That is to say, it must make judgments as to what programs and issues merit consideration by the legislature, but at the same time, it must reduce to manageable levels the volume of information that is communicated.

The culmination of the fiscal staff's review is a report of its budget analyses which it submits to the legislature several weeks subsequent to the presentation of the *Governor's Legislative Budget Message*. The report is still a relatively new feature of the overseeing function and has a limited distribution, which includes primarily members of the Ways and Means Committee in each house, though other individual legislators may obtain copies on request. In any event, it is treated as an internal document to facilitate the overseeing function of the Ways and Means committees; and therefore, by establishing its own communication network directly with state agencies and generating in the process a report that is independent of the *Governor's Budget Report*, the legislature reduces its dependence on other elements of the task environment in the performance of its overseeing duties.

Rules and regulations. Unlike the developing communications networks between the legislative organization and other state agencies with respect to budget review, no well-developed communications system exists for reviewing agency rules and regulations. As with any matter that is recommended for passage by the legislature and that is to have thereafter the effect of law, rules and regulations must take the form of a technical instrument of communications. To ensure that they are in proper form, the regulations must be submitted to the Attorney General's Office for review. Since rules and regulations are supposed to carry out legislative intent, the more crucial question, it would seem, is how well the legislative organization communicates its intent through the passage of legislation.

The establishment of a communications network would be expected to accompany the development of the emerging technology in performing this task. The development of such a system has been advanced by recent efforts of the legislature to improve its performance in this area. During the 1976 interim, the Legislative Coordinating Council established, for the first time, the Special Committee on Administrative Rules and Regulations, which was charged with the responsibility of making recommendations on proposed changes of the rules to the standing committees that would consider them during the session. Other interim committees had made recommendations for improving this overseeing function, as had the committee also, but no other committee had offered recommendations on the proposed changes in the rules and regulations themselves.

In fulfilling its charge, the Special Committee on Administrative Rules and Regulations solicited testimony from agency representatives, thus establishing, if only temporarily, a direct line of communications between state agencies and the legislature. The committee also expressed concern over the lack of participation on the part of those individuals and groups in the environment who would be affected by changes in state regulations. As a result of that concern, the committee recommended that state agencies publicize more effectively the public hearings required in the review process and that they thereby encourage greater input from environmental elements. If successful, then, the developing communications system will be extended to include linkages with affected groups and individuals in the environment, as well as those within the organization.

Audits. The directional flow of communications in the audit function of the emerging technology differs somewhat from that which exists in the process of overseeing agency budgets and regulations. Most communications in the audit function occur within the task environment between state agencies and the legislature, and only at key points do they intersect the lawmaking process. To begin with, communications in the performance of the audit function flow outward, away from the legislative organization. Unlike communications in the other overseeing functions, the budget review begins with the submission of state agency budget requests to the legislature; and in like manner, state agencies submit proposals for changes in the rules and regulations. But communications in the audit function initially take the form of a directive to the postauditor from the Post Audit Committee, which provides information concerning the matters in the performance audit that the committee feels merit attention. The directive constitutes the primary form of communication of a formal nature between the legislature and the postauditor.

Communications that support the audit function generally parallel the form that the performance of the function assumes—that is, they are intensive. Since the performance audit is conducted selectively, it has a limited duration, which is subject, of course, to the variables, among others, of the size and function of the agency and the purpose of the audit. Communications between the Division of Post Audit and the audited agencies, therefore, have not been regularized and are not routine. However, a more enduring line of communications would be expected to develop with the agency audit, since an audit of each agency must be conducted every two years.

Communications during the performance by the audit staff itself are especially direct, involving a close examination of agency records, as well as personal interviews with agency personnel. Given the concentrated and direct communications associated with the process and given the fact that the audit function is often considered an exact discipline, one might anticipate that the information that is communicated would be routine and unquestioned. But such is not always the case, as is evidenced by recent audits, including that of the state treasurer. It is especially interesting to note the exchange of communications between the agency and the Division of Post Audit, as well as others, because they tend to gravitate away from specifics and from the technical nature of the audit and its findings toward the value-laden generalities of the political arena, centering on the expressive communications that arise between independent agencies of the executive branch of government and the legislative organization.

The final phase in the communications system of the audit function is the reporting of its findings and the making of recommendations to the legislature for implementation. These are communicated by way of an independent audit report, which can be classified as a type of informational communications. But, as in all other proposals and recommendations that seek to become law, the nontechnical information that is provided must be translated into the technical language of the system, a function that the Revisor of Statutes Office performs, as discussed previously. The bills are subsequently assigned to appropriate standing committees for consideration. The postauditor or his designated representative may be requested to testify before a standing committee; however, no established link has developed between the Division of Post Audit and standing committees on the same order as that with the Post Audit Committee.

Federal government. Since federal legislation and rules and regulations have a significant impact on the operations of state government, some communications linkage is required in order to maintain a current record of federal action that affects the state. That information concerning federal authority is most frequently communicated through state agencies. They are the ones that are affected most directly because of their role as implementers. In addition, they possess the time and the necessary resources to devote to a study of the intricacies of federal legislation and regulations so as to determine their full impact on the state and the functions of their agencies. In implementing a federally sponsored program, the federal government often insists that the governor or appropriate state officials designate a single state agency to serve as coordinator of a program, so that communications concerning implementation of that program can be directed to that agency without creating a number of confused, mixed, or overlapping lines of communication between the federal government and several agencies in various branches of the state government.

Intraorganizational Communications

The intraorganizational communications in the emerging technology do not differ appreciably from those in the dominant technology, because both are concerned directly with the lawmaking process. The only differences are those which might inhere in the functioning of the Ways and Means committees or in committees that review rules and regulations.

Both Ways and Means committees, for example, make extensive use of subcommittees in reviewing agency budgets. Since most subcommittees meet with agency representatives in the course of their review, a direct line of communications, however brief, is thereby established. Committee members are not, therefore, wholly dependent on the *Governor's Budget Report* or the fiscal staff's budget analyses for their information.

Another source of information related to the review of agency budgets is a communicative instrument that summarizes committee action (including that of the Committee of the Whole) on appropriations bills. Termed a "bill explanation," it is the functional equivalent of a fiscal note for an appropriations bill. It contains essentially two kinds of information: committee expenditure adjustments to the governor's recommended budget and a narrative explanation of the expected impact on agency programs. Just as fiscal notes are updated as bills are amended, the bill explanation is changed to reflect the adjustments of additional amendments as the appropriations bills proceed through the lawmaking process.

With respect to intraorganizational communications in the reviewing of rules and regulations, it should be noted that legislation was introduced during the 1977 session to create a permanent standing committee for the purpose of reviewing rules and regulations. If this or similar legislation should eventually become law, the developing communications network, which currently branches out to encompass all committees that review regulations, would be narrowed and strengthened by channeling all communications to a single committee, which would make this aspect of the overseeing technology its sole function.

PART 3

Socialization

In order to function effectively, every organization must devise some method for ensuring compliance among its members with the goals and procedures it has established for itself. Large industries characteristically have a formal, institutionalized process of orienting their employees to the operations of the organization, an oftentimes intensive process, which may persist for a period of several months or more. The nature of the legislative organization precludes a rigid, routinized method of this sort but substitutes methods of its own, both formal and informal. Nor is the legislator socialized to perform a single role. A legislator must play the role of representative to his constituency; he must also observe organizational norms, remain loyal to his party, adhere to the social norms attendant to his status in the legislature (distinctive especially in the Senate), and maintain and defend his own integrity as an individual.

Once again, Etzioni, in providing a rudimentary taxonomy of types of compliance, establishes a basis for describing and analyzing the forms of socialization as they exist in the Kansas legislature. The three types of compliance that he identifies in organizations are normative, utilitarian, and coercive.² Socialization of the type described above, which Etzioni would classify as utilitarian, differs from that found in the legislative organization. Members of utilitarian organizations owe the initial and continued status of their membership to elements within the organization—that is, to management. Members of the legislature, in deriving their membership from outside the organization—that is, from the voters in their respective districts— have fewer obligations to leaders in the organization. Consequently, compliance in the legislative organization is determined in large measure by forces outside the organization as well as within it.

Extraorganizational Socialization

Etzioni makes a further distinction between instrumental and expressive socialization. Instrumental socialization is described as training, whereas expressive socialization is characterized as "education minus training." Socialization influences of an extraorganizational nature are primarily of the expressive variety. That is to say, they embody the prevailing values of a democratic society. Inasmuch as the legislature is an organization that is expected to be a microcosmic reflection of the interests that it seeks to represent, it is obliged to structure its organization and rules of procedure in conformance with those same principles which exist in society at large. As a result, the legislative organization more nearly resembles an organization of the normative type.

Foremost among the norms that the organization internalizes for adoption by its members is that of equality. Each member is entitled to cast but a single vote on any given issue. Opportunities to introduce legislation, offer amendments, and engage in debate are made, for the most part, without regard to membership in any party or faction.

The process of socialization in those organizations which demand a rigid compliance with organizational goals risks stifling creativity in the organization. As noted previously, compliance is usually sought by elements within the organization, whether by leadership or by peers. By requiring a rigid adherence to the rules, the original goals of the organization may be lost, and compliance, as a goal in itself, may be substituted. The healthy interplay between the individual and the organization could mean that an individual whose efforts must be directed exclusively to "fitting in" cannot be expected to manifest any real creative energies when, if by chance, he subsequently assumes a position of leadership. The legislative organization, however, with its periodic elections and consequent influx of new members on a regular basis, is largely spared the potentially dysfunctional consequence. Moreover, the democratic norm that seeks to protect the integrity of the individual also militates against such an eventuality.

The legislator may buffer his dependence on environmental influences by the type of role that he assumes. The candidate who is running for public office more nearly resembles the description of a "delegate,"[3] a posture that is dictated by the nature of the campaign. But the enfranchised decision-maker, having gained membership in the legislative organization, may become disposed to view his role as that of a "trustee," especially if some disparity is seen to exist between the legislator's personal predispositions about an issue and the general feeling of his constituency. This permits a greater degree of latitude for the individual legislator than would otherwise occur during the campaign in respect to the expression of personal ideas and feelings. To that extent this buffers the legislator from personally unacceptable environmental inputs, while it does not, at the same time, abandon democratic principles. The strength of socialization in the organization is revealed in its capacity for developing between legislators an allegiance to the organization whose strength and endurance can rival, and at times supercede, a legislator's dependence on any single segment of the environment.

Intraorganizational Socialization

Formal processes. The legislative organization has several formal mechanisms that serve to orient its members to the procedures by which the organization functions. These would qualify as techniques of instrumental socialization. The Institute for State Legislators, which was jointly sponsored by the Kansas legislature and the Capitol Complex Center of the University of Kansas in November 1975 and again in November 1976, afforded legislators the opportunity of examining their role in the legislature and of offering recommendations for improving the legislative process. Legislators who participated thereby lay the necessary groundwork for the acceptance of change which constitutes an indispensable part of the success of any measure of reform.

Another formal instrumental process of socialization is the rather cursory orientation session that precedes the commencement of each legislative session. The orientation meeting is designed primarily to acquaint new members with available staff services, and it is conducted largely by representatives of legislative staff agencies, including the Legislative Research Department, the Revisor of Statutes Office, the Division of Post Audit, the Legislative Reference Library, Legislative Administrative Services, and the legislative counsel. In addition, representatives of the news media participate, as does an occasional lobbyist. New legislators are also familiarized with the legislative process by engaging in a small-scale mock legislative session.

Within the organization, the internalization of norms that have evolved in order to make the organization function has taken several forms. There is, for example, a formal set of rules, in addition to *Robert's Rules of Order*, which governs the conduct of members in each house. The complexity of the rules is perhaps indicative of the complexity of the organization, making acceptance of the rules all the more significant to the effective operation of the organization. In a sense, the acceptance of a set of rules establishes the limitations of socialization in many organizations and in the legislative organization as well. It is also means-oriented, to the extent that it works toward the acceptance of a set of principles by which the organization operates, without dictating the content of the final product. To be sure, the goals to which the rules are intended to lead may be enumerated and accepted, but they must be stated in general terms. For example, one goal may be that all legislation that is passed must benefit the public interest.

The quality of being means-oriented can likewise be attributed to the acceptance of democratic values. In a circumstance where differences are not only tolerated but are structurally supported, a workable proposition is an agreement to disagree.

As noted previously, the norm of equal treatment, which has its origin in the environment, takes a formal, institutionalized form in the rule that there shall be one vote per member. But norms of an informal nature also operate within the organization. The norm of equal treatment, for example, has several informal manifestations.

Informal processes. The strength and endurance of such a norm is especially evident when it is examined in relation to efforts for reform. Included in the recent suggestions for reform of the legislative process is one designed to remedy the problem, experienced each year, of the introduction of a flood of bills, many of which will never receive a favorable recommendation from the first committee. The proposed remedy is to limit the number of bills that an individual legislator may introduce in a given session. But the remedy runs counter to the established practice of a legislator's presumed right to introduce legislation as he deems desirable. The same may be said of efforts to limit debate or to expedite questioning in committee in the interest of time. In most cases where a measure of reform obtrudes upon the province of a legislative norm, even if it is designed to enhance the efficient operation of the organization, the latter will more often prevail.

Other informal, unspoken norms may be found in the legislative organization: keeping promises, willingness to compromise, the avoidance of personal remarks in the course of discussion. Legislators are usually given preference over other nonlegislative conferees who appear before a committee for the purpose of submitting testimony on a bill that the committee has begun to consider. Legislators are seldom refused when making an appeal late in the session for a committee to introduce legislation. Similarly, a motion offered in committee, even though it has no chance of success and is supported only by its author, will seldom die for want of a second. Another norm ensures that the committee member making the motion will be given the opportunity of explaining it to the committee, inviting discussion as a result of the explanation, and submitting it eventually to a vote by the full committee. Such a norm exists not only for the benefit of a minority, even a minority of one, but for the majority as well. It yields the benefit to the majority of having considered all sides in the course of its deliberations, a strategy that makes the ultimate decision appear to be the result of careful, deliberate, and fair consideration.

Leadership. It has already been observed that legislative leaders do not occupy the same position of authority and control as do their counterparts in private industry. Unlike management, then, they do not have a significant impact on the form and content of socialization processes in their organization. Much of the reason for this difference has been attributed to the normative nature of the legislative organization. The prevailing norm of equality, for example, precludes the imposition of a rigid hierarchy and a well-developed formal process of socialization to perpetuate it. Because most of the socialization pressures exerted on members within the organization are informal and because of the flat structure of the organization, these measures constitute a pattern of informal interaction among members which is characterized as "peer pressure." Notions about the attitudes and behavior that legislators are supposed to assume are preserved and perpetuated by other legislators.

The behavior of leaders appears to be no less subject to these pressures. Certain attitudes and modes of behavior are expected from anyone occupying these positions. The president of the Senate and the Speaker of the House are, as leaders of a large organization, expected to defend the organizational integrity of the legislature when it is criticized by the governor, interest groups, or others. Similarly, as party leaders, the president and the Speaker are expected to uphold party positions on major issues. Committee chairmen are expected to justify the action taken in their committees, at least insofar as the legislation acted upon was given due consideration prior to such action. With the institutional, administrative, and party roles of leaders reasonably well defined, it might be more accurate to conclude that legislative leaders are socialized into their roles as much as members are socialized into theirs.

Socializing staff. It should not be expected that the processes of socialization are limited exclusively to the membership. As indicated in the first chapter on participants, the legislative employees perform a variety of functions in support of the organization. Their commitment to legislative goals must be regarded as an indispensable ingredient of the successful accomplishment of those goals. Socialization bears less significantly on the performance of tasks by clerks and retainers, though that does not diminish the importance of those functions, because they are somewhat removed from the sensitive areas of policy-making, where the pressures toward behavioral conformity to certain prescribed rules is greatest. Administrators and professionals of certain staff agencies, on the other hand, are obliged to work with the information upon which policy decisions are based; and they develop, as a consequence, a level of expertise in some areas that could influence the outcome of policy decisions, thereby usurping the role of the legislators.

To avert the danger of that possibility, professional employees have assumed the neutral role characterized by the concept of "neutral competence." The concept assumes that staff can function independently of partisan differences between members, that it can provide information to all factions and individuals as requested, and that it can refrain from offering recommendations and personal observations on matters about which it is knowledgeable. To be sure, the processes that work to socialize professional and administrative staff with this attitude are not formal. Rather, they are applied informally among peers over a relatively short period of time.

Critics of what is perceived by many to be the excessive power of a burgeoning bureaucracy are doubtful of the merits of the neutral competence concept. It must be conceded that the nature of human behavior precludes an exact application of the concept in actual practice. The suggestion made in chapter 3—that one function of the Revisor of Statutes Office, for example, is to find solutions to policy questions—tends to support this view of the bureaucracy. But a fair assessment of the concept must include more in its evaluation than a strict adherence to the neutral attitude as it is theoretically conceived. The concept of neutral competence would seem to provide a workable basis for clarifying roles and for establishing relations between legislators and staff.

Linkage between Communication and Socialization

There is some degree of interaction between the networks of communication and the processes of socialization, which tends to reinforce the effective operation of both as supportive technologies. As legislators are socialized into the norms and procedures of the organization, they are likewise socialized into the use of the organization's various communicative devices, a form of instrumental socialization, and the parliamentary language and legislative jargon that characterize debate, a form of expressive communications. Conversely, communication among legislators is necessary in order to transmit feelings and attitudes from one to another so that they can adopt the prevailing behavioral norms of the organization. Thus, these two supportive technologies, in addition to supporting the primary technologies of the organization, support each other as well.

PART 4

Communication, Socialization, and the Legislature

The communications networks and the socialization processes are influenced in their development by features that characterize the legislature as an organization. Most of those features tend to reduce the effectiveness of communication and socialization processes, even as they develop and expand their supportive functions to accommodate changes in the primary technologies. The organizational characteristics that have had the most significant bearing on the formation of these supportive technologies follow.

1. *Size.* With 165 legislators and over 500 employees, the size of the legislature alone ensures that the networks of communication between individuals will be complex. The division between chambers, as well as those between parties, factions, and staff agencies, further adds to the complexity of communications networks. Expressive communications are the ones that are affected most by size and complexity, particularly those involving debate by the Committee of the Whole. Since all members are equally entitled to express a view on all matters under consideration, discussion is often a ponderous process, even with the elaborate set of rules that has been formulated to govern it. Socialization is likewise affected because of the difficulty in getting large numbers of individuals to comply with any set of norms.

2. *Heterogeneity.* A factor related to size is the heterogeneous composition of the legislature. The differing backgrounds of legislators and the interests represented by constituencies and interest groups ensure a divergence of opinion on all major issues. For that reason, expressive communications are again the ones that are most affected. Heterogeneity is probably a more important factor bearing on the process of socialization in the legislature, because conformance with a given set of norms suggests a measure of behavioral uniformity—a difficult goal to achieve in an organization with as much institutionalized diversity as there is in the legislature. The factors of size and heterogeneity both influence expressive socialization processes more than instrumental ones.

3. *Specialization.* Through its use of the committee system, the legislature specializes by encouraging committees to develop some degree of expertise on matters related to a particular subject area, such as education, welfare, and so forth. The legislature specializes further by dividing the function that it performs into the traditional lawmaking technology and the emerging overseeing technology. The development of the fiscal section in the Legislative Research Department and of the Division of Post Audit to assist the legislature in the performance of its overseeing function is further evidence of specialization

in the legislative organization. Accordingly, special communicative devices, as described earlier in this chapter, have been developed and utilized in a complex, multidimensional network of communications to parallel the internal structure of the organization. The translation function of legislative staff agencies serves the additional purpose of preventing specialized functions within the legislature from becoming too narrow and antonomous; this is done by translating technical and detailed actions in committee, for example, into nontechnical language which can be more readily understood by all.

Specialization also affects socialization processes in a general sense to the extent that legislators accept the committee system as a workable method by which legislation can be considered and to the extent that the emerging overseeing technology is accepted as a legitimate function of the legislature. In a more specific sense, some legislators and staff members, in addition to their other roles, are also socialized into the role of "expert" and serve as key resource persons in their respective areas of expertise.

4. *Time.* No other factor among those mentioned has as much impact on the functioning of both communications networks and socialization processes as does time. The time factor, as it relates to expressive communications, centers primarily on the lengthy, time-consuming nature of discussion and debate in committee or in Committee of the Whole. Unlike the influence of time on expressive communications, the effect on instrumental communications has not received much attention. For example, as a bill is amended and passed out of committee with a favorable recommendation, the Revisor of Statutes Office is responsible for drafting a committee report, which must be formally adopted by the Committee of the Whole. The majority floor leader is unable to schedule the bill for debate on general orders until this technical instrument of communication has been prepared.

The same is true of a bill explanation compiled by the fiscal section of the Legislative Research Department on appropriation bills. Though not requiring formal adoption by the Committee of the Whole, a bill explanation is used by the floor manager of an appropriations bill (usually the chairman of the Ways and Means Committee), and it must be prepared in advance of debate before the full membership of either house. Consequently, this form of communication also possesses the potential for delaying action on a bill. Throughout most of the session, delays go unnoticed because there is other work to be done while communicative instruments of this sort are being prepared. But during the waning hours of the session, it becomes very apparent how crucial such documents are to the legislative process when all other work is finished and the legislative staff agencies work under acute time constraints to prepare them.

Expressive socialization processes have been identified as being more prevalent in the legislative organization than are instrumental processes. Given its formal, osmosislike nature, expressive socialization yields its best results over an extended period of time. Since the legislature is in session for only a quarter of each year, there is a limited amount of time for this kind of socialization to work.

The impact of problems resulting from these organizational factors can to some extent be reduced. Computerization, for example, has aided the communication of information generated as a result of legislative action. One such network of communication, the bill-locater system, has reduced the complexity of the history of legislative action on bills to manageable proportions by making access to the information instantly available to those who possess the proper input code on a computer terminal. But other changes that could mitigate the negative influences of these organizational factors are resisted by the democratic norms, among others, which are identified in the first part of this chapter. Expressive communications, which are subject to the greatest amount of distortion, are affected most by these norms. They ensure, for example, that all opinions are voiced, regardless of the time that it takes or the number who wish to be heard. They may even contribute to the problem of distortion by encouraging the use of catchwords that will have the maximum political effect but will disguise the true meaning of the messages that are communicated. Thus, communications during debate have, to a large extent, acquired the reputation of having only a symbolic meaning, while the communications that facilitate the making of important decisions are believed to be informal, direct, and relatively free from distortion.

Whereas the democratic norms may have a somewhat adverse effect on the effective operation of some communications systems in the legislative organization (which only confirms that the legislature is essentially a normative organization), those same norms may tend to offset the negative aspects of the organizational factors on socialization by serving as a basis for agreement on rules governing organizational behavior. The strength of the commitment to those norms is of sufficient intensity to provide a workable level of consensus and stability to a largely nonhierarchical, environment-dependent organization.

The argument of part 3 of this chapter is that several identifiable features of the legislature as an organization are directly related to the structure and effectiveness of communications systems and socialization processes and, further, that the prevailing norms governing behavior in the organization, in their interaction with those features, both help and hinder, in varying degrees, the functions of the supportive technologies.

9
Change in the Kansas Legislature

The modern legislature, an invention of the seventeenth century, was created to perform two interrelated tasks—those of representation and of legitimation. In other words, the legislature was to be the democratic institution in its role as elected representative of the voting public. The legislature was also conceived as an institution that would serve to protect against the concentration and unwarranted use of power. James Madison, in *Federalist 51*, makes the point:

> To what expedient, then, shall we finally resort for maintaining in practice the necessary partition of power among the several departments as laid down in the Constitution? The only answer that can be given is, that as all these exterior provisions are found to be inadequate, the defect must be supplied by so contriving the interior structure of the government as that its several constituent parts may, by their mutual relations, be the means of keeping each other in their proper places.[1]

The legislature and its environments have changed substantially since the 1600s, as has the environment for all of government. These changes are reflected in the changing role of the legislature. Some, however, have argued that the legislature has not been able to adapt as well as has the executive.[2] Others have suggested that the legislature has become secondary in power to the executive.[3]

But legislatures, we argue, have been and are changeable, adaptable institutions. They are much like other forms of organizations which are sensitive to changes in their environments. Like other organizations, legislatures are responsive to uncertainty, while at the same time attempting to control uncertainty. Perhaps the reason that many students of legislatures think of legislatures as unchanging is that from some perspectives—for example, the study of facets of the legislature—legislatures indeed appear to be resistant to change.

In the case of the Kansas legislature—as well as other legislatures—it may be that not only has the legislature changed but it has changed substantially. The perspective that we use to view both the Kansas legislature and changes in it is one of organization theory. A perspective of organization theory defines the legislature as an organization—as a series of interrelated parts—that is constantly adapting and attempting to control external uncertainty. As we stated in the beginning of this chapter, legislatures were created to protect against the unwise use of power. In other words, legislatures were created to be *political institutions*. As they have evolved, however, legislatures have become something more than political institutions. Modern democratic societies require not only that legislatures preserve the democratic system but also that they respond to problems. Thus, legislatures, which were constructed as democratic institutions, have also had to become problem-adapting institutions. In other words, the Kansas legislature has also become a *political organization*—organization in the sense of structuring itself to collect information and personnel so as to adapt to and/or solve problems.

But what is the cause for these changes in the Kansas legislature? Samuel Huntington has suggested that political change, in part, is a function of the increasing diversity and complexity of society.[4] We suggest that Huntington's notion of change is also applicable to organizations and that it is specifically applicable to the Kansas legislature. Moreover, we suggest that the growing diversity and complexity of Kansas society have put additional pressures on—or have caused uncertainty for—the legislature in its attempts to resolve some of the problems of the state. If Huntington's theory is applicable, these additional pressures should have led to changes in the legislature as an institution. To test the validity of the proposition that legislatures have changed as a result of changes in society, we need to examine how the environment of the Kansas legislature has changed since 1861.

PART 1

Diversity and Complexity

Like the rest of the United States, the state of Kansas has changed substantially since 1861, the year that Kansas was admitted to the Union. One indicator of change has been the growth of the state's population, which has been steady since the tremendous growth in the 1870s and 1880s and has only been interrupted during the decade from 1930 to 1940 (table 9.1). The most significant change in the state's population has not been in its growth, however, but in where the population lives. Table 9.2 shows the shift from an overwhelmingly rural to a predominantly urban state.

Historically, one of the major responsibilities of state government in terms of expenditures has been to support state and local education. As the population in Kansas has grown and become predominantly urban, there has been a significant increase in the number of high-school graduates and an increase, until the last few decades, in the percentage of children in the 5–21 age group who are enrolled in school (table 9.3). The most telling figures, however, of the increasing financial commitment of the state (and the legislature) to education are the expenditures for education that have been made from the state's General Fund. The original Kansas Constitution established

TABLE 9.1

POPULATION GROWTH IN KANSAS AND THE UNITED STATES, 1870–1975

Year	Population Kansas	Population U.S.	Kansas Population, as percentage of U.S. Population
1870	364,339	38,558,371	0.94
1890	1,428,108	62,979,766	2.27
1910	1,690,949	92,228,496	1.83
1930	1,880,999	123,202,624	1.53
1940	1,801,028	132,164,569	1.36
1950	1,905,299	151,325,798	1.26
1960	2,178,611	179,323,175	1.21
1970	2,249,021	203,810,000	1.10
1975	2,314,479	213,137,000	1.09

SOURCE: *Kansas Statistical Abstract* (Lawrence: Kansas University Institute for Social and Environmental Studies, 1975), p. 3.

TABLE 9.2

URBAN AND RURAL POPULATION OF KANSAS, 1870–1975

| Year | Population | | Percentage | |
	Urban	Rural	Urban	Rural
1870	51,870	312,529	14.2	85.8
1890	269,539	1,158,569	18.9	81.1
1910	492,312	1,198,637	29.1	70.9
1930	729,834	1,151,165	38.8	61.2
1940	753,941	1,047,087	41.9	58.1
1950	993,220	912,079	52.1	47.9
1960	1,328,741	849,870	61.0	39.0
1970	1,484,870	761,708	66.1	33.9
1975	1,751,000	606,000	74.3	25.7

SOURCE: *Kansas Statistical Abstract* (Lawrence: Kansas University Institute for Social and Environmental Studies, 1975), p. 3.

TABLE 9.3

CHILDREN (AGES 5 TO 21) ENROLLED IN PUBLIC SCHOOLS

Year	Number	Total Population, Ages 5 to 21	Percentage Enrolled
1870	63,218	109,244	57.9
1890	391,420	509,614	76.8
1910	398,915	516,061	77.3
1930	432,749	555,080	78.0
1940	365,970	487,546	75.1
1950	337,416	456,740	73.9
1960	455,165	615,286	74.0
1970	502,462	740,349	67.9
1975	465,355	....	......

SOURCE: State Department of Education, State of Kansas Statistical Annual Reports.

state aid to local school districts through the Annual School Fund. But as table 9.4 shows, state support has increased dramatically in recent years.[5]

The state's contribution to support of local schools changed substantially in 1965 with the passage of the School Foundation Finance Act. This law was enacted in recognition of the fact that the reliance of local school districts on ad valorem taxes could not keep up with

TABLE 9.4

EXPENDITURES FOR EDUCATION FROM THE STATE GENERAL FUND

Year	Amount Spent for Education	Total of General Fund	Percentage Spent on Education
1920	$ 2,758,000	$ 8,972,238	30.7
1930	3,609,000	10,652,943	34.2
1940	8,112,000	20,870,110	38.9
1950	24,471,000	66,701,364	36.7
1960	59,495,000	117,817,053	50.5
1970	214,887,000	343,628,784	62.5
1975	356,705,000	598,390,705	59.6

NOTE: In 1966 the Sales Tax Revenue Fund was combined with the General Revenue Fund. The figures for the years before this date have been adjusted by incorporating the figures for the Revenue Sales Tax Fund as found in the 1969 Kansas Financial Report and the state audit reports for the other years. The 1920 and 1930 figures are as they stand because no Revenue Sales Tax Fund existed then. The 1970 and 1975 figures are from the governor's Annual Budget Message.

the increasing demand for educational services and with increasing costs.[6] The state's tax base was wider, and it also reflected the growth of personal and corporate wealth.

As the population has shifted from rural to urban, the economic base of the state has also shifted. The diversity of the state's economy can be seen in two trends: in the shift away from agriculture as the dominant employment base and in the increasing diversity of employment. Using only agriculture, manufacturing, and government employment as indicators of the trends, the changes are marked (table 9.5). Agricultural employment (although not the wealth derived from agriculture) decreased, from 59.1 percent of total employment in 1870 to 8.3 percent in 1975. According to 1975 census figures, the largest employment sector in Kansas was wholesale and retail trade, which accounted for 18.4 percent of all employment.[7] This shift represents the evolution to a more complex economic system. Evidence of this shift and of its effect on state government can be seen in the change in the state tax base and in expenditures from the General Fund by the legislature.

Prior to 1926 the largest source of state revenues was a state property tax. During that period the state property tax accounted for approximately one-half of all state operating revenue.[8] By 1968 it accounted for only 1.42 percent of all state operating revenue. In

TABLE 9.5
EMPLOYMENT SECTORS IN KANSAS, 1870–1975

Year	Agri-culture	Percentage of Total Work Force	Manufac-turing	Percentage of Total Work Force	Govern-ment	Percentage of Total Work Force
1870	73,228	59.1	18,726	15.1	....	......
1890	256,582	56.7	54,674	12.1	....	......
1910	274,246	44.1	114,953	18.5	9,994	1.6
1930	229,340	33.0	131,715	18.9	12,062	1.7
1940	183,515	31.4	53,071*	9.1	23,361	4.0
1950	171,300	23.6	95,300	13.2	80,500	11.1
1960	112,200	14.5	116,000	15.1	115,000	14.9
1970	78,200	9.3	134,500	15.9	154,000	18.3
1975	83,400	8.3	159,600	15.8	170,500	16.9

SOURCE: U.S., Bureau of the Census, *Census of the Population*, occupations sections.
* The Census Bureau changed the definition of categories.

1925 the state enacted a tax on gasoline, all the revenues from which were earmarked for the state or counties (80 percent) and cities (20 percent).[9] In fiscal year 1925 the state spent $120,111 on highways. In fiscal year 1926 the amount jumped to $7,859,959, an increase from 0.77 percent to 33.31 percent of total state expenditures.[10] In 1937, expenditures for highways and other transportation amounted to 64.5 percent of all state expenditures; in the history of Kansas, this was the largest portion of the state budget to be spent for any one area.[11] (A significant percentage of the state's total operating revenue by the 1950s came from federal grants, as shown in Table 9.6.)

In 1933, Kansas voters amended the constitution to allow income taxes. In 1937, primarily because of declining revenues and increased demands due to the Depression, the state legislature enacted a 2 percent sales tax. An example of the use of the additional revenues was the Kansas Social Welfare Act of 1937, which, through matching federal funds, established a comprehensive welfare system in Kansas. As a result, total state spending for welfare jumped from $341,865 in 1937 to $4,387,614 in 1938.[12]

The major increase in funding for local education occurred in the mid 1960s, when the legislature increased the state aid to local school districts. State funding for education increased from $29.5 million in 1960 to almost $215 million in 1970, an increase from 49.1 percent to

63.1 percent of expenditures from the state's General Fund.[13]

Changes in overall expenditures from the General Fund are shown in Table 9.7.

Politically, Kansas has also become more diverse. Kansas has historically been a one-party state. In the state legislature this has certainly been true, but beginning in the 1960s, the Democratic party has become more powerful (table 9.8). In the 1977–78 session, for the first time since the 1913–14 session, the Democrats controlled the House. The Senate was controlled during the 1977–78 session by the Republicans by a narrow 21 to 19 edge.

The state of Kansas has become more politically and economically diverse. The increase in population and its shift to urban areas, along

TABLE 9.6

FEDERAL GRANTS TO KANSAS STATE GOVERNMENT, 1915–75

Year	Amount	Percentage of Total State Operating Revenue
1915	$ 116,348	2.21
1925	303,617	2.06
1950	37,587,230	20.84
1960	94,136,295	26.25
1970	201,901,484	37.25
1975	335,366,000	25.92

SOURCES: James Drury, *The Government of Kansas*, rev. ed. (Lawrence: University Press of Kansas, 1970), p. 164; and State of Kansas, Annual Budget, 1970, 1975.

TABLE 9.7

EXPENDITURES FROM THE KANSAS STATE GENERAL FUND, 1920–75

Year	Amount
1920	8,972,238
1930	10,562,943
1940	20,870,110
1950	66,701,364
1960	117,817,053
1970	343,628,784
1975	598,390,705

SOURCES: State of Kansas, Annual Budgets and the governor's Annual Budget Report.

TABLE 9.8

PARTY AFFILIATION IN KANSAS LEGISLATURE BY PERCENTAGE, 1870–1977

	House			Senate		
Year	Republican	Democratic	Other Affiliation	Republican	Democratic	Other Affiliation
1871			(No data available)			
1891	20.8%	5.6%	73.6%	95.0%	2.5%	2.5%
1911	59.2	40.0	0.8	87.5	12.5	
1931	60.8	39.2		92.5	7.5	
1941	78.4	21.6		87.5	12.5	
1951	84.0	16.0		85.0	15.0	
1961	66.4	33.6		80.0	20.0	
1971	65.6	34.4		80.0	20.0	
1975	57.6	42.4		65.0	35.0	
1977	48.0	52.0		52.5	47.5	

SOURCE: State of Kansas, Senate and House Journals.

with the decline in agricultural employment and the growth of employment in more urban-oriented business and in government, have reflected this diversity. In addition, this diversity is seen in changes in state expenditures and changes in the tax base that are necessary in order to support the increased expenditures. But more important to the legislature, the changes that have occurred in Kansas have presented the legislature with a more complex and thus a more uncertain environment.

Uncertainty

The more diverse and complex the state has become, the more complex and uncertain the issues that confront the legislature have become. The more urbanized and business-oriented the state has become, the more economic health has become dependent on a stable economy—an economy stabilized at least in part by the actions of government. The upheavals caused by economic problems such as those that occurred in Kansas in the 1890s and 1930s are shown by an increase in legislation in the late 1890s and the out-migration of population in the 1930s. Both problems resulted in greater demands upon state government—demands for government help to those who were unemployed or otherwise adversely affected, which translated into a demand for new revenues for state government at a time when other sources of revenue were bringing in fewer dollars. Demands for welfare, which were directed at state and local government, were borne entirely at the state and local level in the early 1930s. The intervention of the federal government into welfare through the Social Security Act of 1935 did not alleviate uncertainties for the state legislature. (The federal legislation made grants to the states on a matching basis.) The state legislature found itself committed to policies and funding that were not always controllable by the legislature.

A more complex, industrialized society that depends on specialized skills increases the demand for a variety of educational resources. Education has become the major area of expenditures for state and local government. By 1974, 39.5 percent of state expenditures and 49.5 percent of local expenditures were used to support education.[14] In 1974, those expenditures amounted to almost $1 billion ($985,547,000), of which $97,836,293 from the state's General Fund went in support of the seven public institutions of higher education under the Board of Regents (including the University of Kansas Medical Center). Almost 14 percent of the amount appropriated for higher education goes to the University of Kansas Medical Center.

The other two major areas of state expenditures—namely, highways and public welfare—are also the result of a more complex state economy. The need for highways is integral to the survival of an agricultural and manufacturing economy. Since the gasoline tax was enacted, monies derived from it have been earmarked for road construction and maintenance. The advent of significant federal grants

TABLE 9.9

EXPENDITURES FOR EDUCATION FROM THE KANSAS STATE GENERAL FUND, 1920–75

Year	Amount
1920	$ 2,758,000
1930	3,609,000
1940	6,187,000
1950	11,471,000
1960	29,465,000
1970	214,887,000
1975	356,705,000

SOURCES: State of Kansas, Annual Budgets and governor's Annual Budget Message.

for highways in the 1950s brought about significant increases in spending for highways and a host of other responsibilities for state government—from policing the highways to maintaining rest areas along the major interstate freeways.

Expenditures for public welfare, as mentioned previously, were in part a response to the Depression and to federal legislation requiring state policy and fund-matching. Changes in the economic health of the state and the eligibility requirements have led to substantial increases in expenditures from the state's General Fund (see table 9.10). (Reliable figures exist only as far back as 1954.)

The enlarged responsibility and greater uncertainty that the Kansas legislature has faced have also been affected by actions of other political organizations. For example, in the last ten years the Kansas legislature has been changed substantially in its membership by the United States Supreme Court's decision in *Baker* v. *Carr*, which required that both houses of state legislatures be apportioned according to population.. The Supreme Court's decision affected the Kansas legislature in terms of its representative base; it also created the problem of how to comply with the decision. In another instance, the California Supreme Court, in *Serrano* v. *Preist*, has mandated that the California legislature provide more equitable financing for local school districts. The decision does not directly affect Kansas, but it does raise the possibility of similar litigation in Kansas.[15]

The Changing Role of the Kansas Legislature

The economic, social, and political changes in Kansas have brought about a changing role for the legislature. An increased demand for services and for variety of services has made government,

TABLE 9.10

EXPENDITURES FOR WELFARE FROM THE KANSAS STATE GENERAL FUND, 1954–75

Year	Amount
1954	$14,334,000
1960	15,689,000
1970	46,056,000
1975	97,355,000

SOURCES: State of Kansas, Annual Budgets and governor's Annual Budget Message.

and the legislature, more involved in areas that traditionally were left to local government or to the private sector. An enlarged tax base has added to the changes by providing the resources that the legislature must have in order to be able to respond to demands. The evolution of sales and use taxes and income taxes, which in FY 1976 constituted 34.1 percent and 31.8 percent of all state revenues in Kansas,[16] have also fueled change, because they reflect—although not proportionately—the growth of the state's economy. This form of taxation is fraught with uncertainty, however, for general economic activity can decrease as well as increase the tax revenues. Thus, the legislature constantly has to cope with the uncertainties of revenues from sales and income taxes, which can fluctuate from month to month.

The state budget in Kansas has grown considerably since 1861, especially in the last five decades. This growth has marked an extension of the legislature's sphere of influence. Perhaps the best example of this extension is the increasingly active role of the legislature in overseeing the executive branch. The reasons for this more active role may be explained in part by the increasing size of state government, as is seen in the number of state employees (see table 9.11) and the more complex and uncertain environment for the administration and for the implementation of legislation. The complexity of legislation, the necessity for administrative discretion, and the size of state bureaucracy have required that the legislature devote more of its time and resources to overseeing.

TABLE 9.11
AVERAGE NUMBER OF KANSAS STATE EMPLOYEES, 1942–75

Year	Classified	Unclassified	Classified Exempt	Total
1942	8,640	3,124	......	11,764
1950	9,907	3,804	108	13,819
1960	15,690	8,015	431	24,136
1970	21,755	15,974	225	37,954
1975	24,754	18,198	239	43,191

SOURCE: State of Kansas, Personnel Department, Department of Administration.
NOTE: Classified employees include most of the employees of the state and are those positions under the jurisdiction of the state's Personnel Department. Unclassified positions are numerous because they include many upper-level civil servants along with all academic positions in the state colleges and universities. The exempt positions are exclusively political appointments. For further explanation, see Kansas statutes SS75-2935 and SS75-2935a.

In summary, the legislative environment in Kansas has changed substantially since the Kansas legislature was founded. The changes have become more intense in the last five decades. The changes have resulted from a much more complex social, economic, and political society; consequently, more complex issues or conflicts have come to the legislature for resolution. The issues confront the legislature with greater uncertainty about revenues, about what solutions exist for problems that may lie outside the control of the legislature, and about the administration and implementation of the decisions that the legislature does make. According to Huntington, society responds to diversity, complexity, and uncertainty by becoming more complex in order to be more independent and more adaptable and yet to retain some coherence over time. The next section of this chapter is a study of how the Kansas legislature has changed in response to a changing society.

PART 2

Response to Diversity and Complexity

In a study of the United States House of Representatives, Nelson Polsby concluded that democratic legislatures adapt to complex environments and tasks through the process of institutionalization. By institutionalization, Polsby meant that legislatures have had to become more independent entities that are more differentiated from their environment. Legislatures have also had to become more complex through greater specialization of subparts of the legislature and through greater division of labor among committees. Legislatures also have created staff, procedures, and recruitment patterns that give greater coherence to the legislature and to legislative behavior.[17]

Polsby's assumptions about the reasons for changes having occurred in the House of Representatives were based on the overall increase in social, economic, and political complexity and the resultant need for a more viable organization. Over its century of existence the Kansas legislature has had to evolve from a relatively uncomplicated, homogeneous environment to a complex, increasingly urban-industrial one. To what extent has the Kansas legislature changed so as to cope better with a more diverse and complicated society?

One way that the Kansas legislature has adapted to greater complexity in society and in policy issues has been to improve the way the legislature passes laws—the dominant technology—and to improve the resources necessary to make the technology as rational as possible through information-gathering processes—searching and learning processes. In order to accomplish the improvement of these two processes, the Kansas legislature has had to become a more complex organization in two respects: through a division of labor of the members and through a division of labor by means of legislative staff. In other words, the legislature has become a more coherent deciding institution through the establishment of a committee system and staff agencies such as the Revisor of Statutes Office and the Legislative Research Department.

In the early years of legislative activity, the most prevalent process for decision-making was to conduct most, if not all, business through the Committee of the Whole (i.e., the whole membership sitting as a committee). This procedural system was used extensively by the United States Congress and by the Kansas legislature in their first years of existence and is still used in both houses of the Kansas legislature. In the early years of the Kansas legislature, committees were established to hear and deal with proposed legislation, but they were not used extensively. As the Kansas legislature has evolved and as the number of bills introduced has increased, the legislature has found that, as in other organizations, a division of labor becomes an efficient way of accomplishing work. The relationship is shown by comparing the number of bills introduced during a session of the legislature with changes in the number of committees. For example, to cope with the sizable increase in the number of bills introduced in 1891, the number of committees in both houses increased substantially (see table 9.12).

The number of committees in both houses increased until the last fifteen years. The recent years have reflected the increased reliance upon committees to accomplish the work of the legislature. As a result, fewer committees are preferable to a great number of committees that have little purpose or work.

The committee system in the Kansas legislature has evolved into an extensive system for dividing the labor of the members and for developing/relying on committees. The utilization of committees is not as equitable as it might be. Members of both houses have expressed concern with the present division of labor, which tends to favor certain members and committees.

As part of the division of labor, the leadership of both houses of

TABLE 9.12

NUMBER OF LEGISLATIVE COMMITTEES AND NUMBER OF BILLS INTRODUCED

Year	Number of Committees		Number of Bills	
	House	Senate	House	Senate
1871	26	25	415	143
1891	49	32	854	420
1911	54	39	1,067	687
1931	37	44	687	410
1941	42	46	525	403
1951	42	29	598	307
1961	44	32	489	408
1971	23	17	643	421
1975	19	15	640	606

SOURCE: State of Kansas, Senate and House Journals.

the Kansas legislature is critical to the effective performance of the institution. Although leadership positions have always been necessary to the legislature, these positions have presently become more meaningful in regard to the management of the legislature. The two most important positions are the president of the Senate and the Speaker of the House. Both have evolved into almost full-time jobs, with salaries larger than those of other members, because of the necessity for maintaining leadership the year around. Both positions have small personal staffs that provide the resources for the president and the Speaker to keep track of the members and the issues during the session and the interim. The majority and minority leaders of both houses are also paid more than other members, and they have small staffs. One of the characteristics of the institutionalized Kansas legislature is that positions of leadership evolve which have special responsibilities (discussed in more detail in the latter part of chapter 7) and which serve a substantial percentage of the members. One indication of this trend is the institutionalization of minority-party leadership with a support staff, both of which participate in the management of the legislature. (These leadership organizations will be discussed later in this chapter.)

The Kansas legislature is not a full-time organization, nor is the members' principal occupation that of being legislators. This system seems to be adequate for meeting the needs of the state and for conforming to the dominant view that the legislature should be a "citizen legislature." Because of its part-time nature and the strong tradition that there should be a regular turnover of members, the legislature has developed differently from the United States Congress. In Congress, members, once elected, tend to stay for extended periods of time and to leave only if they are not reelected, if they are elected to a higher office, or if they are prevented from serving again because of personal reasons. Members of the Kansas legislature do not usually remain in the legislature for long periods of time.

The concept of a citizen legislature is complemented by a number of factors that have helped to establish the tradition of a citizen legislature. First is the low compensation for members. Not all legislators can afford to spend three to four months in Topeka each year, away from their regular jobs, and still prosper. This factor may be a significant reason for the substantial turnover of the legislature in every biennium. Second, the lack of appreciation and interest of the members in the legislative process is a major reason for members deciding not to run for reelection.[18] The lack of appreciation and interest may be aided by the fact that state legislators do not have high status as compared to those in other professions. In addition, before reapportionment, some Senate districts rotated the seat among counties. This practice led to turnover at every election. Third, for those who have political ambition, membership in the state legislature is not an end but rather a means to higher political office. Members of the state House of Representatives regularly retire to run for the state Senate, and members of both houses use their positions to run for statewide or congressional offices.

In the period 1954–66 the turnover in the Senate was 57 percent of the total membership every four years. In the House the figure was somewhat lower, 44 percent every two years. Of those who did not return to the legislature, only a small proportion were defeated in reelection attempts.[19]

In spite of the high turnover in both houses, the legislature has still been able to maintain continuity and to draw upon the specialization of members who have returned for additional terms. For example, in the House, which has traditionally had longer service from members than has the Senate, during the 1975–76 session there were twenty members each of whom had ten or more years of service. The average number of years served by a member of the House has been around seven years. This figure has been relatively constant since reapportionment. In the Senate in the 1975–76 term, only three members had

TABLE 9.13

MEAN* NUMBER OF YEARS SERVED BY KANSAS LEGISLATORS, 1871–1975

Year	House	Senate
1871	2.6	....
1891	5.4	2.5
1911	5.1	3.3
1931	5.6	3.6
1941	5.8	4.1
1951	6.7	5.3
1961	7.3	4.7
1971	7.1	6.8
1975	7.4	6.0

SOURCE: State Library, Individual Legislator File.
* Mean computed through ungrouped data technique.

over ten years of service; and six was the average number of years served, which also has remained constant since reapportionment. Table 9.13 shows the increasing continuity in the Senate and the House from 1871 to 1975. The mean number of years served has been increasing in spite of reapportionment, the changes in party competition, and the tradition of substantial turnover.

The Kansas legislature meets for approximately four months (January through April) in odd-numbered years and for about three months (January to March) in even-numbered years. But the tradition of a part-time legislature has not always met the needs of the state. In 1933, the legislature created the Legislative Council, which was to function as the legislature's representative arm during the interim between biennial sessions. It was made up of the leadership of the two houses and functioned as an interim organization for administration and research into problems for the next legislative session. This council was created in recognition of the fact that the part-time legislature could not keep up with the legislature's business during the interim, nor could it effectively research the problems facing the state and propose solutions for the consideration of the entire legislature. The specific responsibilities of the Legislative Council's charge were covered in the legislation:

> It shall be the duty of the council to collect information concerning the government and general welfare of the state, examine the effects of previously enacted statutes and recommend amendments thereto, deal

with important wide interests, and to prepare a legislative program in the form of bills or otherwise . . . to be prepared at the next session of the legislature.[20]

The creation of the Legislative Council as a specialized arm of the legislature was in part related to the environment in Kansas in the 1930s. (In addition, the creation of the Legislative Council recognized that the federal legislation attempting to cope with the Depression required a response from the Kansas legislature prior to the legislative session in January 1935.) The new Congress, elected in 1932 along with President Roosevelt, reacted to the Depression with an unprecedented variety of legislation, most of which required matching legislation on the part of states in order to be implemented. The new session of Congress adjourned on 16 June 1933, and the Legislative Council, the first of its kind in the country, met on 15 August 1933, to frame the Kansas legislature's response to the federal laws. Of the proposals that were formulated by the Legislative Council in 1933 and 1934, a good number dealt with various pieces of federal legislation— public works construction, the National Employment Service Act, the Home Owners Loan Act, the Federal Emergency Relief Act, and the Federal Banking Act of 1933. In addition, the Legislative Council developed legislation to implement the National Industrial Recovery Act (NIRA), which offered grants to the states that would cover 30 percent of labor and materials for public-works projects to hire the unemployed. During the 1933–35 council session, fifty-four bills were considered and drafted by the council.[21]

The evolution of the Legislative Council in Kansas reflected two changes. By the early 1930s the legislature's task of lawmaking required that the legislature give some interim consideration (research) to legislation that was to be considered in the next session. The legislature was finding it helpful both to conduct more research in dealing with legislation and to participate in setting the legislative agenda.

Making the new Legislative Council work required the help of additional staff. The staffs that have evolved in the legislature are of two kinds. There are members of the professional staff, the desk staff, who, for example, deal primarily with the technical aspects of the legislative technology. Examples of the technical duties are bill-drafting, bill analyses, and general management services. The other professional staff members are concerned primarily with policy questions— for example, auditing the implementation of legislation and providing general research services.

Not only has the legislature had to adapt to external complexity, but also the lawmaking task within the legislature itself has been made much more complicated by the number and complexity of bills introduced each session. The number of bills introduced has led to changes in resources and procedures of the legislature. The desk staffs provide the resources to cope with the increase of the number of bills introduced in each house. The desk staffs, which are under the direction of the secretary of the Senate and the chief clerk of the House, make the legislative technology work. Members of the desk staffs constituted the first staff of the legislature. They make sure that the constitutional and statutory requirements concerning proper introduction of bills, readings, passage, and transmittal are handled correctly. The staffs also keep the records of legislative action and follow legislation throughout the lawmaking process. The desk staffs are the primary resource necessary to implement the legislative technology and to coordinate the activities of the two houses.

The desk staffs are necessary because of the limitations on the time and skills of the members. The increase in the number and complexity of pieces of legislation has meant that the Kansas legislature has had to draw upon other sources for information, expertise, and management. The Kansas legislature, like many other state legislatures, has in the past depended on other organizations for necessary skills. Lobbyists, for example are a form of staff, in that they provide information. However, they are not the most objective in their information. The Kansas legislature has opted to establish its own indigenous staffs as being more predictable and objective sources of information and expertise.

After instituting the desk staffs, the legislature did not employ any sizable staff until 1929, when the Revisor of Statutes Office was created. It was created at the recommendation of the Kansas Bar Association, primarily because the compiling of legislative statutes before 1929 was left to private means, which were unpredictable and not well organized.[22] In addition to making a compilation of statutes and revising it after each session, the Revisor of Statutes also helped the legislature in the drafting of legislation and in advising the members about legal language and its ramifications. The latter duty resulted from the need for legislation to be better written and researched. The Revisor of Statutes Office was not originally a part of the legislature. As first established, the Revisor of Statutes was appointed by the Supreme Court, although it was designed primarily to serve the legislature. This arrangement changed in the early 1970s, when a legislative Office of Revisor of Statutes was created. The Revisor's Office gave the legislature its own full-time staff for legal advice and for performing the critical function of compiling and devising the increasing number of statutes passed by the legislature. The compiling task is critical, because the court system is dependent upon an accurate, up-to-date code, which is referred to regularly by lawyers and judges.

In 1934 another staff organization was created to help in the gathering of information for lawmaking—the Research Department of the Legislative Council.[23] Although a part of the Legislative Council, the Research Department was funded for its first three years by the Spelman Fund of New York City, a philanthropic endowment which was interested in improving legislatures and legislative staff. The Research Department at first employed only two professionals and relied upon additional help from graduate-student summer interns (one of whom in the summer of 1938 was a student from the University of Kansas by the name of Elmer Staats, who is presently the comptroller general of the United States).

The legislature was struggling with the problems of the Depression and the federal legislation designed to mitigate it at the time that the Research Department was created in the summer of 1934. Legislation at the state and federal levels was designed to reduce unemployment and reconstruct a viable economy. But the proposed legislation confronted the legislature with the dilemma of finding new sources of revenue to replace those lost by diminishing economic activity and to fund the new state and federal programs. One of the first research projects of the Research Department was the investigation of a state sales tax as a possible source of revenue. The research required that the state know both the amount of revenue that could be raised and the consequences to Kansans of having to pay this tax.

In addition to reacting to the Depression and federal legislation, the Research Department was a source of information about ongoing problems in the state. In his first report to the Legislative Council, Fred Guild, the first director of the Research Department, cited the staff's study of public-school finance as a major research effort. School finance has always been a problem to legislatures, in that members are always concerned with its ramifications to their constituents. The problem is often compounded by the fact that when reform is suggested, no one knows exactly what the ramifications will be. In Guild's report to the Legislative Council, he cited the role of the Research Department in dealing with this problem:

> A tentative school-finance bill was drafted on a basis to secure financial data as to how the bill would affect the various school districts through-out the state. . . . A large portion of the Department's [research] time was consumed in a detailed application of the proposed school finance bill.[24]

The Research Department was to collect the information so that all the members could evaluate the effect of a school-finance bill on their constituencies. To legislate solutions to long-standing problems is no small matter.

In its first few years the major responsibility of the Research Department was to assist the members of the Legislative Council in matters of research. This research was directed to general problems that were given to the department for study. A review of the "Reports and Recommendations to the Legislative Council" provides a good outline of the activities of the Research Department. In 1934, in addition to public-school finance and the sales tax, the department worked on a new code for state corporations, measures concerning flood control and conservation, and a whole series of bills related to federal legislation (NIRA, the Federal Home Owners Corporation, and others). In its 1936 report, the department cited work on general sources of revenue and on social-security legislation. The department's research on social-security legislation was sent to the legislature on 16 August 1935, the day after it was signed into law by President Roosevelt. The Research Department's activities on social-security legislation received national attention as an example of research enabling the legislature to respond quickly and efficiently to federal legislation.[25]

As the specialized research arm of the legislature, the Research Department has changed considerably since its inception. These changes have been the result of the increasing specialization required in order for the legislature to perform its legislative task. In 1934 and immediately thereafter, the principal task of the Research Department was to look into and provide reports about current problems and/or specific recommendations for legislative consideration. As it has since evolved, the Research Department has greatly added to these functions. The general research orientation, which results in detailed research reports, has given way to other responsibilities. The department now provides staff for special, select, and standing committees of the legislature during both the session and the interim. As part of the staff's responsibility, members of the department act as research agents for the committees and the committee chairmen. In general, the research role of the staff of the Research Department has been greatly extended. Because of these many responsibilities, however, the resources of the Research Department have increasingly been directed to immediate research requirements rather than to long-term problems of the legislature.

There are exceptions to the trend toward more immediate research needs of the legislature. The Research Department's fiscal staff is an example of a staff that focuses on many of the long-term complex issues that the legislature faces. Its major responsibilities are to estimate changes in state revenue brought about by fluctuations in the state's economy and to estimate revenues from suggested new state tax sources. The latter task necessitates the complex job of investigating the total impact of federal spending in Kansas and the ramifications of changes in policy regarding federal block grants, categorical grants, and revenue-sharing.

The postauditing function for the state was performed until 1971 through the statewide elected office of state auditor in the executive branch of the state government. Until the office of state auditor was abolished in 1972, most of the responsibility for the overseeing of legislative monies and policies was accomplished through that state-elected office. In order to better control postaudit responsibilities, the legislature created the Division of Legislative Post Audit in 1971, which is under the control of the Joint Post Audit Committee. The legislature's action in effect transferred a majority of the state auditor's responsibilities to the legislature.

The creation of the Division of Legislative Post Audit recognized the need for the legislature to have adequate resources for overseeing the implementation of public policy. But the creation was also a recognition that postauditing had become more complex than just the accounting of monies appropriated by the legislature. By 1974 the postaudit responsibilities had become as much program audit as finance audit;[26] that is, postaudit was responsible for overseeing the implementation and performance of legislative policy in addition to the accounting of monies. The growing interest in controlling the postaudit functions of financial and policy auditing mirrors the greater complexity of state government. The technology of the legislature has been extended to overseeing the operations of the executive branch.

The overseeing responsibility is necessary because uncertainty exists in the bureaucracy with regard to the process of administration and implementation. Thus, the Post Audit Division has become more crucial to the legislature's ability to oversee. The increased responsibility of the division is indicated by the fact that thirty-five professionals are employed in the office, making it the largest (professional or full-time) staff office in the legislature.

As the legislature has become more complex and diverse, there has been a need for technical-management staff to oversee the administration of the legislature. The desk staff oversees the administration of the lawmaking process—the legislative technology. As the legislature has changed and as staff organizations have been created, the administration of the legislature has required more resources. Up until the 1930s, most of the administrative responsibilities—such as hiring and paying temporary employees during legislative sessions, arranging full payment of members, and other duties—were performed by the leadership. With the creation of the Legislative Council in 1933, most of the administrative responsibilities fell to the council's secretary, the revisor of statutes. For a time in the 1930s and 1940s a good part of the administrative responsibilities was performed by the director of the Research Department. After secretarial staff and offices were provided to the members of the legislature in the mid 1960s and because of the growing technical and professional staff, the legislature in 1969 created the Joint Committee on Legislative Services and Facilities. The Joint Committee's responsibilities included the establishing of uniform pay standards for employees of both houses and the coordination of services.

Two years later, the legislature created the Office of Legislative Administrative Services. The director of this office is responsible to the Legislative Coordinating Council. The responsibilities of this office are to oversee the purchase and maintenance of legislative equipment and supplies, to maintain payrolls and reimburse expenses for members and staff, to recruit and supervise temporary personnel during a session, and to maintain meeting rooms, reports, and minutes of committees. A special administrative office of the legislature is a reflection of the administrative responsibilities brought about by a greater number of legislative employees and the resultant increases in the size of the legislative payroll.

The Office of Legislative Counsel was created in 1974 to give the legislature a greater voice in certain legal matters. For a number of years prior to 1974, the legislature was controlled by the Republicans, although the attorney general, who was elected statewide, was a Democrat. This partisan difference led to opinions from the attorney general that had political ramifications with which the leadership of the legislature disagreed. In order to provide a more balanced interpretation to correct this situation, the legislature created its own office to represent the legislature in legal matters. In addition, the legislative counsel acts as advisor to members on legal questions relating to the legislature and, on request, acts as counsel to committees in investigatory situations. Immediately after its creation, the Office of Legislative Counsel was active in representing the legislature in reapportionment matters.[27]

Legislative Reference, a part of the State Library, is the data-reference organization for the legislature. Legislative Reference and the State Library are maintained in the Statehouse and are an integral part of the resources necessary for the functioning of the legislature and its staff offices.

Since its inception and especially since 1929, the Kansas legislature has found it necessary to create various staff organizations to help the legislature carry out its tasks. These staff organizations have made the legislature a more complex institution that is better able to cope with the complex and often unanticipated issues that the legislature must attempt to resolve. The more complex system of staff and committees of the legislature has helped to create a more independent legislature. Over the last five decades the legislature has lessened its reliance on other organizations—specifically on lobbyists and the executive branch—to help it recognize, resolve, and oversee problems. Members of the legislature now have their own staff, which is available to aid them in technical or professional problems, and have personal secretarial staff to respond to communications from their constituents. The Research Department furnishes the legislature with estimates of state revenue to help determine total amounts for the state budget.

The evolution of a more complex system of committees and staff has also brought about other changes that have led to the institutionalization of the Kansas legislature. The research, audit, revisor, counsel, and administrative offices, along with access through legislative committees, have meant more access on the part of all members of the legislature to staff resources. Access to staff resources is by no means equal, but the Kansas legislature has made substantial improvements by having rules that apply universally. In the words of one legislative leader, "the evolution of staffing resources has benefited the minority party as much as the majority party, perhaps more."[28]

Many of the newer members of the legislature complain about the closed nature of Senate and House leadership and about the small number of committees used for important legislation. However, as the number of terms served by members of the legislature increases, as it has been doing in the past few years, the rules governing the selection of leadership and referrals to committees should become more equitable. The increase in the number of terms served by the members and the presence of legislative staff give coherence to an institution that requires some continuity and stability in order to learn, to collect information, and to decide. Modern organizations and modern legislatures have to be somewhat coherent in order to survive matters concerning school finance, general taxation, and a host of other subjects that come before the legislature. The Kansas legislature is competing with lobby groups, the executive branch, and other organizations which have relative stability. Other organizations do not meet for three to four months every year and then virtually disband.

The institutionalization of the Kansas legislature has been marked by the legislature's becoming a more complex, autonomous, and coherent organization. The late 1960s and early 1970s have indicated this trend. The increase in terms served has resulted in greater continuity in number and leadership. The establishment of the Division of Legislative Post Audit, the legislative appointment of the revisor of statutes, the creation of a fiscal staff in the Research Department, and the establishment of offices and secretarial help for the members have made the legislative organization more complex and have made the legislature a much more adaptable, autonomous organization.

Legislatures are supposed to be democratic. At the same time, legislatures are supposed to be responsive, to attempt to solve complex problems faced by society that are brought to the legislature for resolution, and to be able to change.

The Kansas legislature, constructed in the image of seventeenth-century legislatures, has had to change in order to adapt to the changes in the environment. It has had to change in order to perform its job of lawmaking and making authoritative decisions. No other institution can perform these tasks. And the Kansas legislature, like other democratic legislatures, has accomplished this adaptation by becoming institutionalized—by becoming more independent, more adaptive, and more coherent. It has evolved from a political institution into a political organization.

10
Assessment

The Kansas legislature has evolved from a political institution into one that is both an institution and an organization. The more the legislature's tasks of lawmaking have become complicated and complex, the more the legislature has come to rely on improved information and expertise, which are supplied through suborganizations established by the legislature. At the same time, more complicated and complex tasks have changed the legislature's technologies by requiring modification in lawmaking procedures and by stimulating the development of instruments for overseeing the operations of the executive branch. Environmental changes are connected to organizational changes through activities of evaluation.[1] The Kansas legislature, like all democratic legislatures, undergoes a constant process of assessment. Internally, different factions or parties are continuously assessing the activities of other factions. Externally, lobbyists, local governments, the governors, and constituents are assessing the actions of the legislature. The legislature (members, leaders, staff) and the legislature's environment (lobbyists, constituents, courts, governor) are constantly constructing "score cards" that assess how well the legislature is performing.[2]

Frank Thompson defines a score card as "a device which expresses in abbreviated and generally quantitative form how well an individual or group is performing." But as Thompson points out, "Where one stands depends upon where one sits."[3] How one assesses the legislature depends on what one's preferences are regarding performance. Those who closely observe the Kansas legislature (namely, the governor, lobbyists, parties, executive departments) assess the legislature in terms of particular preferences about policy. The inattentive public, or those people in Kansas who do not follow the legislature's behavior closely, assess the legislature in terms of actions that affect them directly (increase in taxes) or in terms of the response to a legislator acting as an ombudsman for a problem that they are having with state government. Legislators themselves assess their legislative performance in terms of influence to pass certain favored legislation or in terms of the number of bills introduced by them that become law.

Obviously the legislature cannot be all things to all people. It cannot perform well on every scorecard or under all assessment criteria. What we suggest by examining the Kansas legislature from a framework of organizational theory is that the assessment criteria used by the legislature have changed as the nature of the legislature has changed. One way to examine the change in the way that the legislature assesses itself is to look at the different sources of assessment, on the one hand, and the type of legislature that is being evaluated, on the other.

PART 1

Institutional and Organizational Assessment

As we stated earlier, legislatures are constantly being assessed by external and internal sources. At the same time, internal and external assessments are being made about two aspects of the legislature—the legislature as a political institution and the legislature as a political organization. Chart 10.1 may make this point understandable. Where the assessment is internal and the criteria are institutional, the standards are usually associated with partisan advantage or disadvantage (A). The majority party attempts to pass legislation that will be advantageous to that party, while the minority party establishes points of opposition that it hopes will serve as political ground on which to build a majority. Where the assessment is external and the criteria are institutional, the standards are usually policy outputs (B). Did

CHART 10.1

TYPE OF LEGISLATURE
BEING ASSESSED

		Political *Institution*	*Political* *Organization*
	Internal	A	C
SOURCE OF ASSESSMENT			
	External	B	D

the legislature pass the legislation that was preferred or valued? Did the legislature perform well in terms of a variety of legislation that met the expectation of, for example, the Kansas Farm Bureau, state government employees, or any other group?

Where the assessment is internal and the criteria are organizational, the standards of assessment (C) are related to how efficiently the legislature functions as an organization. Internal assessment is in terms of the amount of information that is available, the size and quality of the professional and technical staff, and the ability of the legislative technology to work—in other words, for the lawmaking process to perform well. Where the assessment is external and the criteria are organizational, the standards of assessment are often standards of efficiency (D). The standards of efficiency are the number of bills passed during a session, the number of bills considered in committee, the amount of legislative time spent in committee work, and the professionalization of legislative staff, measured in terms of experience and number of advanced degrees.

The internal and external assessments of the Kansas legislature as a political institution are based on norms that expect the legislature to be a constantly changing governmental instrument, one that is responsive to the changing preferences of the citizens of the state and to the variety of economic, social, and political preferences of organized segments of society. The emphasis on policy along partisan lines assumes that the important criteria by which the legislature should be assessed are its responsiveness and its ability to resolve conflict. The indicators of performance—how well the legislature is performing its job—are in terms of the ability of individual members of the legislature, the parties, and the legislature itself to adapt.

The internal and external assessments of the legislature as a political organization are based upon different norms. These norms indicate how well the legislature is performing its functions of gathering reliable information; hiring and retaining qualified staff to make the technology work well; and overseeing policy through the processes of administration and implementation of policy. The information-gathering process and the act of making the legislative technology operational require continuity among the members of the legislature and with regard to their service on committees. Continuity is necessary so that the legislature can learn and can develop the expertise necessary for the technology to deal with complexity.

As the Kansas legislature has changed, it has increasingly been assessed and has assessed itself as a political organization. Two current examples serve as illustrations—one where assessment was made by an external organization, the other involving the legislature's assessment of itself.

In 1971 the legislature was studied by the professional staff of Legis 50 (formerly the Citizens Conference on State Legislatures) as part of an overall study of all of the fifty state legislatures. The Legis 50 study was supposed to assess how well the Kansas legislature was doing in relation to the other state legislatures and to suggest specific changes for improving the legislature's ability to make laws. The Legis 50 study recommended a number of changes for the legislature in the following four areas.

Legislative sessions and processes. Legis 50 suggested a number of changes related to legislative sessions. Restrictions on the length of sessions should be ended, and the legislature should have the ability to call itself into special session. Legis 50 also suggested increased compensation for members, passage of strict legislation dealing with conflict of interest, and strict regulation of lobbyists.

The report on the Kansas legislature also recommended changes in legislative processes. The report suggested that there be joint rules governing both houses, bill summaries for the members, and a statement of intent by the author of each bill and that the legislature establish its own audit function.

Committees. Legis 50 suggested a number of changes regarding committees. First, the number of committees and committee assignments should be reduced. Facilities for committees should be improved, and committee meetings should be open and publicized—including the recording of roll-call votes.

Staff. Legis 50 recommended a general strengthening of legislative staff, especially staff for leaders, rank and file members, and committees.

Facilities. The report suggested that the legislature provide office facilities for individual members and more space for the press and that it improve the support facilities, such as libraries and other facilities for professional and clerical staff. The report also proposed that the legislature establish an office in Washington, D.C., in order to better inform the legislature of changes originating in the federal government.

All of the recommendations of Legis 50 were designed to improve the legislature's ability to become a more efficient organization. The recommendations did not directly address improving the quality of its output. The changes suggested infer that better procedures, better staff, and better facilities lead to a legislature that is beter informed and more independent, and thus a legislature that should be able to make better decisions.

The legislature responded to a number of the suggestions made by Legis 50. The legislature now has the capability of calling itself into session; the staff at almost every level has been enlarged; offices and clerical staff have been established for members; audit responsibility has been established under the legislature, with a sizable increase in staff; and in general, a substantial change in legislative processes and facilities has been accomplished. These changes led Legis 50 to designate the Kansas legislature for the legislative improvement award in 1976.

In 1974 the Legislative Coordinating Council authorized a legislative institute to meet every year for the purpose of providing members with an opportunity to meet and discuss a series of general and specific topics. The second session, held in the fall of 1976, focused on assessment of four dimensions of the legislature: the lawmaking process; the overseeing of the executive branch; research and administrative services; and leadership. The agenda for the 1976 institute was constructed by the leaders and senior staff members of the legislature.

The lawmaking process. Discussion at the institute centered on different aspects of the lawmaking process. The members considered the efficiency of the agenda-setting process. They were concerned about the time they spend on insignificant bills, time taken at the expense of developing major pieces of legislation.

Some members of the Kansas legislature thought that more effort should be given to inviting testimony from a larger cross section of society. In addition, there was a general concern that chairmen and members of committees do not make adequate use of the staff in the decision-making process.

Legislative overseeing. The legislature's assessment of overseeing was concentrated into two areas—budget and audit. In Kansas, the legislature does not prepare its own budget. It works from a budget submitted by the governor. The general concern of the legislators was that they could improve substantially the processes used to review and evaluate the governor's budget. Most of the changes that were discussed related to increasing the time for consideration of the budget, incorporating a much larger time perspective to the budget process (looking at three- to five-year budget periods, rather than just at the imminent fiscal year), and devoting more interim time of the budget committees to budget monitoring and implementation.

The audit responsibility of the Kansas legislature has expanded substantially in the past six years. However, members of the legislature were concerned that the audit staff did not have clear directions from the legislature as to a long-term audit strategy and that the legislature in general was not making good use of the audit staff in the overseeing of the operations of the executive branch.

Research and administrative services. The staff available to the leadership, committee chairmen, and members has been enlarged, but there was concern that most members of the legislature are not aware of the staff resources available to them and that staff is used too much on an ad hoc basis and too little toward the development of long-range goals with regard to legislative policy. The legislators concluded that increasing the number of staff persons is not an answer to legislative problems, that staff increases should be accompanied by the development of policies on the use of staff. For example, the legislators debated to what extent legislative research staff should be more concerned with overall analysis of policy and less concerned with analyses of all bills that are introduced and referred to committee.

Administrative services were the subject of assessment because of the increasing pressure for services associated with responding to constituents (such as committee hearing rooms, the size of committee rooms, the availability of legislative documents) and for increased services for the members (offices, clerical staff, parking space). Administrative services are of special interest to legislators because they affect the public image of the legislature.

Leadership. The focus of most of the discussion on leadership was on the power of the leaders—should the powers be continued or should they be curtailed. At issue was the access of the members to assignments on interim committees. The Coordinating Council decides who will serve on interim committees, and it also assigns topics. A number of the members expressed a preference for a more open process of selection that would facilitate introduction of legislation considered by an interim committee. This more open process could be accomplished through appointment of standing-committee personnel to posts on interim committees.

In summary, assessment of the Kansas legislature involved two general assessment values. One emphasized change and responsiveness[4]—the legislature as a political institution—where the evidence of the legislature's performance is assessed in terms of its ability to respond to change. The other perspective of the assessment emphasized stability and coherence—the legislature as a political organization. The latter approach defines good performance as the ability of the legislature to gather the information necessary to make reasoned decisions, to employ professional and technical staff who extend the ability of the legislature to decide and to perform the complex task of overseeing.

The evolution of the Kansas legislature has involved both change/responsiveness and stability/coherence. But in terms of assessment, the evolution has meant that the legislature's assessment of itself has become more important in determining how the legislature should change as an organization and what stability is necessary for the legislature to be able to perform its tasks. The changes in the past ten years support this conclusion.

Since the mid 1960s the Kansas legislature has made a number of significant changes that have come about because of the legislature's assessment of its performance. Individual offices and staff for every member have enabled the legislators to be more responsive to constituents by providing secretarial staff for communications with constituents. The evolution of the Coordinating Council was in response to demands by all the members of the legislature for greater access to interim research and for a more influential role in setting the agenda for the next session. The establishment of the Legislative Post Audit Division acknowledged the greater importance of overseeing to the process of legislative decision-making. The change of the Post Audit Division into both financial and performance auditing is added evidence of the legislature's concern for its own overseeing staff and for greater emphasis on following legislation through to implementation. Following legislation after it has been acted upon by the legislature represents a substantial change in legislative responsibility.

The leadership of both houses of the legislature has become concerned with improving the legislative technology and the supports that make it work. There appears to be less concern about gaining partisan advantage and more concern about access of members to decision-making and to adequate resources. Evidence of these trends is seen in the larger numbers of legislators who are involved in interim committees and the staffing changes that have benefited all of the members. Other evidence of change in leadership is the leadership support of the legislative institute. The institutes have given the general members of the legislature the opportunity to consider changes in legislative operations. In one institute the topic for discussion was the necessity for extended negotiations between leaders and members before the election of leaders.

PART 2

Conclusion

The Kansas legislature has been attempting to improve its learning and searching ability in order to improve its lawmaking technology. The improvements have been directed toward more information and better expertise, more knowledge about the complex and uncertain issues that the legislature is asked to resolve. These improvements have led to increases in staff and to changes in procedure and structure. When viewed from the perspective of a political organization, the changes may be seen as improvements in the way that the Kansas legislature, as an organization, attempts to cope with the complexity of its job. But if the same changes are viewed from the perspective of the legislature as a political institution, they might not be seen as improvements at all.

For example, if we review the legislature's performance in financing secondary and elementary schools during the past decade and a half, we should probably discover a computerized information system and a willingness and ability to demand sophisticated kinds of statistical analyses—both of which suggest significant improvement in the legislature's decision-making capability. But if we inquire into how well the legislature has been able to resolve conflict among contending groups, we might conclude that no important changes have occurred.

The distinctions between the two assessment perspectives is a subtle but important one in understanding the varying perspectives for judging the performance of the Kansas legislature or its component organizations.

Like many other legislatures, the Kansas legislature assesses itself—for the benefit of itself and others—by surrogate standards which James Thompson calls "efficiency tests." These tests measure legislative process by the length of the legislative session, the number of bills introduced and passed, the time spent in committees or on the floor, and other measures. The resources of the legislature are assessed by the number of support staff, by the professional standing of the staff, by the use of technology such as voting machines, and by the level of experience and education of the legislators.

Surrogate standards in assessing resolution of conflict are more difficult to find, a fact that probably explains the relative inattention of the legislature to assessing itself as an institution.

Notes

CHAPTER 1

1. This statement is not meant to disparage the structural and procedural descriptions of legislatures that are presented in such well known treatises as *The Legislative Process in the United States*, by Malcolm E. Jewell and Samuel C. Patterson (New York: Random House, 1966); *The American Legislative Process: Congress and the States*, by William J. Keefe and Morris S. Ogul (Englewood Cliffs, N.J.: Prentice-Hall, 1968); and *The Congressional Process: Strategies, Rules, and Procedures*, by Lewis A. Froman, Jr. (Boston: Little, Brown, 1967), or to ignore the contributions to our knowledge contained in the studies sponsored by the Eagleton Institute of Politics, Legis 50, and the American Political Science Association. The point is that there are few scholarly studies that treat legislatures as "organizations" in the full sense of that word's meaning to organization theorists.
2. James D. Thompson, *Organizations in Action* (New York: McGraw-Hill, 1967), p. 20.
3. Philip Selznick, *Leadership in Administration* (New York: Harper & Row, 1957), pp. 5–7.
4. Thompson, *Organizations in Action*, p. 13.

CHAPTER 2

1. This estimate is based on the breakdown of "manufacturers" in Kansas, by employment; statistics compiled by the Kansas Department of Economic Development.

2. James David Barber, *The Lawmakers* (New Haven, Conn.: Yale University Press, 1965).
3. Robert Presthus, *The Organizational Society* (New York: Knopf, 1962), chaps. 6, 7, and 8.
4. The leaders who plan to stand again for their posts probably want their supporters in the legislatures to seek reelection, but that interest is not the same as an organization's interest in a stable work force of trained employees. Legislators are more likely to provide incentives to keep administrators, professionals, and secretaries than incentives designed to encourage legislators to run for reelection.
5. The Ways and Means Committee, the Committee on the Judiciary, and the Committee on Education are generally considered the major committees in the Kansas legislature. It is assumed, therefore, that the average length of service on these committees is likely to equal that of other major committees and to be higher than that of minor committees.
6. The term "task environment" is attributed to William R. Dill, as discussed in his article "Environment as an Influence on Managerial Autonomy, *Administrative Science Quarterly* 2 (March 1958): 409–43.
7. Marvin Harder and Carolyn Rampey, *The Kansas Legislature* (Lawrence: University Press of Kansas, 1972), p. 208.
8. Though the Kansas Constitution places the office of attorney general in the executive branch, he is an officer of the court and is relatively independent of gubernatorial control.
9. In recent years the office of attorney general has been held by a Democrat. That fact probably influenced Republican legislative leaders to create a staff position that would be occupied by a person who would serve at the pleasure of the leadership.
10. *Statutes of Kansas*, L. 1953, Ch. 375, G.S. 1955 Supp. 75-3701 to 75-3904. The Finance Council was a part of legislation creating a State Department of Administration, which replaced a World War II creation, the State Emergency Fund Board.
11. *State of Kansas, ex rel., Curt T. Schneider v. Robert F. Bennett, Governor, et al.,* 219 Kansas 285. Justice David Prager issued the opinion of the court.

CHAPTER 3

1. Omitted from these categories is the leadership group called the Legislative Coordinating Council. This council could be called an executive committee and treated as a fifth type. But there is only one council in the Kansas legislature, and therefore it would be slightly misleading to suggest that the council is a *type* of committee. For the same reason, the Post Audit Committee has been excluded from this typology.

CHAPTER 4

1. One of the most common terms in the literature of political science is "process." It is generally used to mean all the activities that in one way or another help us to understand how political institutions perform their functions. The ways in which political decision-making is influenced are as much a part of its meaning as the procedures through which decisions are reached. "Process" refers to behavior, whether formal or informal, patterned or atypical, rational or irrational. Nothing is excluded from the meaning of "process," save perhaps the content of political decisions, and even content becomes an object of study by students of process if in any way it may help them to explain how and why certain decisions are made.

2. Implicit in this assumption is the perception of the legislative process as involving a specialization of analytical-judgmental tasks, but not as a monopoly by phase of any activity. This can and does occur at any time. The argument can be made that, given the purposes and characteristics of a legislature, this is functionally necessary. That is, if it didn't occur at one stage, it would have to occur at another.

3. One of the changes that has occurred in organization theory is the recognition of the limitations of the closed-system strategy in studying organization behavior; this has led to a move to open-system strategies (James Thompson's terminology in *Organizations in Action* [New York: McGraw-Hill, 1967]). In essence, an open-system strategy recognizes the dependence of organizations on environmental variables that are not as subject to organizational control as are internal kinds of influences. By task environment, a concept that Thompson attributes to William R. Dill ("Environment as an Influence on Managerial Autonomy," *Administrative Science Quarterly*, March 1958), Thompson means "those parts of the environment that are relevant or potentially relevant to goal setting and goal attainment" (see pp. 27–28).

4. "Buffering," as James Thompson uses the term, means the employment of one or mores devices for protecting an organization's technology from disturbances or uncertainties that impair technical rationality (see pp. 20–21). Here we use the term to denote organizational rules and practices that consciously or unconsciously limit access of interest groups at various stages in legislative decision-making. Buffering has both manifest and latent functions. The rule prohibiting lobbyists from entry to House and Senate chambers during sessions prevents disruptions and delays in lawmaking, but it also limits access to staff and others not affected by the rule.

5. David Easton, "An Approach to the Analysis of Political Systems," *World Politics* 9 (April 1957): 383–400.

6. The leading work on interest-group theory is David B. Truman's *The Governmental Process*, 2d ed. (New York: Knopf, 1971). See particularly chapter 11, "The Dynamics of Access in the Legislative Process."

7. For a brief summary of elite theory see Thomas R. Dye and L. Harmon Zeigler, eds., *The Few and the Many* (Belmont, Calif.: Duxbury Press, 1972), pp. 4–9.

8. For a recent treatment of this and related topics see David R. Mayhew, *Congress: The Electoral Connection* (New Haven, Conn.: Yale University Press, 1974).

9. James G. March and Herbert A. Simon, *Organizations* (New York: John Wiley & Sons, 1958), p. 151.

10. Ibid.

11. Ibid., p. 153.

12. Jeffrey L. Pressman and Aaron Wildavsky have argued that more attention must be given to problems of implementation of policy decisions and that it should occur when policy decisions are being formulated. See *Implementation* (Berkeley: University of California Press, 1973), pp. xii–xvii.

13. The idea of "good workmanship" need not imply "maximizing." It is consistent with "satisficing" as long as the process of reaching a decision accords with the common-sense notion of thoughtful and careful consideration.

14. There is one calendar in the Kansas Senate and one calendar in the Kansas House. They are prepared daily. The House calendar includes the following sections: Reading and Correction of Journal, Introduction of Bills and Concurrent Resolutions, Reference of Bills, Reports of Select Committees, Messages from the Governor, Communications from State Officers, Messages from the Senate, Introduction of Original Motions, Reference of Senate Bills, Motions and Resolutions Offered on a Previous Day, Unfinished Business, Consent Calendar, Final Action of Bills, Bills under Consideration to Concur or Non-Concur, General Orders, Reports of Standing Committees, Bills Adversely Reported, Status of Bills, House Bills in House Committees, Senate Bills in House Committees.

15. In "Organization Theory and the Explanation of Important Characteristics of Congress" (*American Political Science Review* 62 [June 1968]: 518–26), Lewis Froman identified thirteen characteristics of the Congress which he sought to explain by propositions derived from organization theory, particularly from "The Comparative Analysis of Organizations," in James G. March, ed., *Handbook of Organizations* (Chicago: Rand McNally, 1965), and from James G. March and Herbert A. Simon, *Organizations*. Froman's analysis was *causal*, as he explains it; the analysis in part 2 of this chapter is *functional*. The elements of

the lawmaking technology are explained as consequences or functions of the legislature's institutional characteristics.

CHAPTER 5

1. This brief summary of Montesquieu's argument is derived from Franz Leopold Neumann, *The Democratic and the Authoritarian State* (Glencoe, Ill.: Free Press, 1957), chap. 4.
2. One may conjecture that divided political control—a Democratic governor and a Republican-dominated legislature—during the Docking years was an impetus to innovative efforts on the part of Republican legislative leaders to achieve greater independence of the executive office and its instrumentalities. As long as the Republicans controlled both institutions, there was less incentive to legislative independence in the budgetary decision-making process.
3. Martha Derthick, *The Influence of Federal Grants* (Cambridge, Mass.: Harvard University Press, 1970).
4. The opinion of Justice David Prager, in *Curt T. Schneider, Attorney General,* v. *Robert Bennett, Governor of Kansas, et al.,* 1977, I, is an informative, if brief, history of the State Finance Council as well as a brief summary of its previous statutory responsibilities.
5. Graham T. Allison, *Essence of Decision* (Boston: Little, Brown, 1971).
6. Ibid., pp. 32–35, 276–77.
7. For an excellent survey of scholarship related to the problem of bureaucratic responsibility see "Bureaucracies," by Mark V. Nadel and Francis E. Rourke, in vol. 5, chap. 6, of *Handbook of Political Science,* ed. Fred I. Greenstein and Nelson W. Polsby (Reading, Mass.: Addison-Wesley, 1975).
8. Morris S. Ogul, *Congress Oversees the Bureaucracy* (Pittsburgh: University of Pittsburgh Press, 1976).
9. Ibid., p. 182.
10. Ibid., p. 184.
11. Ibid., p. 185.
12. Ibid., p. 195.
13. Ibid., p. 196.
14. Ibid.

CHAPTER 6

1. In the House, the chairman of the Rules Committee is called upon for parliamentary rulings and, in effect, acts as parliamentarian when requested to perform that role.

2. The budget expresses all policy recommendations contained in the legislative message (if appropriations are required for their implementation; appropriations are required for most recommendations) and many more. It is in that sense that the budget is more important than the legislative message.

3. Philip Selznick distinguishes an organization from an institution in the following words: "The organization thus designed is a technical instrument for mobilizing human energies and directing them toward set aims. We allocate tasks, delegate authority, channel communication, and find some way of co-ordinating all that has been divided up and parceled out. All this conceived as an exercise in engineering; it is governed by the related ideals of rationality and discipline. The term 'organization' thus suggests a certain bareness, a lean, no-nonsense system of consciously co-ordinated activities [C. I. Barnard, *The Functions of the Executive* (Cambridge, Mass.: Harvard University Press, 1938), p. 73]. . . . An 'institution,' on the other hand, is more nearly a natural product of social needs and pressures—a responsive, adaptive organism. . . . We usually mean that we are going to pay some attention to its history and to the way it has been influenced by the social environment . . . [and to] how it justifies its existence ideologically" (*Leadership in Administration* [New York: Harper & Row, 1957], pp. 5–6). It is this distinction that suggested the thesis that a sense of an organization as an institution tends to encourage technological innovation.

CHAPTER 7

1. James D. Thompson, *Organizations in Action* (New York: McGraw-Hill, 1967), p. 14.
2. Confidential interview.
3. See *Annual Report: A Report to the Kansas Legislature by the Legislative Post Audit Committee* (Topeka: Legislative Post Audit Committee, 31 December 1976), pp. 1–2.
4. Ibid., p. 1.
5. Ibid.

CHAPTER 8

1. Amitai Etzioni, *A Comparative Analysis of Complex Organizations* (New York: Free Press, 1975), pp. 242–45.
2. Ibid., pp. 246, 249–52.
3. John C. Wahlke, Heinz Eulau, William Buchanan, and LeRoy C. Fer-

guson, *The Legislative System* (New York: John Wiley & Sons, 1962), pp. 272 ff.

CHAPTER 9

1. James Madison, *The Federalist No. 51*, in *The Federalist Papers*, selected and edited by Roy P. Fairfield (Garden City, N.Y.: Anchor Books, 1961), pp. 158–59.
2. Peter W. Sperlich, "Bargaining and Overload: An Essay on Presidential Power," in Aaron Wildavsky, ed., *The Presidency* (Boston: Little, Brown, 1969), p. 171.
3. See Alfred de Grazia, ed., *Congress: The First Branch of Government* (Washington, D.C.: American Enterprise Institute for Public Policy Research, 1966); and Joseph S. Clark, *Congress: The Sapless Branch* (New York: Harper & Row, 1964).
4. Samuel P. Huntington, *Political Order in Changing Societies* (New Haven, Conn.: Yale University Press, 1968), pp. 7–9.
5. James W. Drury, *The Government of Kansas*, rev. ed. (Lawrence: University Press of Kansas, 1970), p. 229.
6. Ibid.
7. *Kansas Statistical Abstract 1975* (Lawrence: University of Kansas, Institute for Social and Environmental Studies, 1976), p. 123.
8. Drury, *Government of Kansas*, p. 149.
9. Ibid., p. 344.
10. James T. McDonald, "Kansas State Expenditures, 1915-1956," *Your Government*, vol. 12, no. 4 (Lawrence: University of Kansas, Governmental Research Center, 15 December 1956), p. 2.
11. Ibid.
12. Ibid.
13. Figures are from *State of Kansas Annual Budget*, 1960 and 1970.
14. Ibid.
15. One case in Kansas has been litigated by the court—*Knowles* v. *State Board of Education* (547 P. 2d 699). The decision is presently under consideration after being remanded to district court.
16. *Kansas Statistical Abstract 1975*, pp. 175–76.
17. Nelson W. Polsby, "The Institutionalization of the U.S. House of Representatives," *American Political Science Review* 62 (March 1968): 144–68.
18. See Bernard L. Barnard, "The Legislature of Kansas: An Appraisal" (Ph.D. dissertation, American University, Washington, D.C., 1949).
19. Ibid.
20. *Laws of Kansas*, 1933, chap. 202, sect. 2.

21. See Barnard, "The Legislature of Kansas."
22. Prior to 1929, Kansas Statutes were compiled by a private citizen, C. F. W. Dassler of Leavenworth, Kansas. See William B. Fenton, *The Office of the Kansas Revisor of Statutes* (Lawrence: Governmental Research Center, University of Kansas, 1965).
23. The Research Department was not created by law until 1921.
24. Frederic H. Guild, *Report and Recommendations of the Kansas Legislative Council* (Topeka, 8 December 1934), p. 13.
25. Ibid.
26. *Annual Report of the Legislative Division of Post Audit*, 31 December 1976, p. 1.
27. See *Kansas Statutes*, sect. 49-1124, for a description of statutory duties.
28. Interview with Speaker Duane S. ("Pete") McGill.

CHAPTER 10

1. James D. Thompson, *Organizations in Action* (New York: McGraw-Hill, 1967).
2. Frank J. Thompson, *Personnel Policy in the City* (Berkeley: University of California Press, 1975), p. 9. See also Herbert Simon, George Kozmetsky, Harold Guetzkow, and Gordon Tyndall, "Management Uses of Figures," in Robert T. Golembiewski, ed., *Public Budgeting and Finance* (Itasca, Ill.: Peacock, 1968), pp. 15–23; and James Thompson, *Organizations in Action*, pp. 83–98.
3. Frank Thompson, *Personnel Policy in the City*, p. 9.
4. These two points are suggested by Nelson Polsby, "The Institutionalization of the U.S. House of Representatives," pp. 144–48.

Index

Administrative Services Office, 96, 104–5, 158
Administrators, 17
Agenda-building, 42–48, 83–84
Allison, Graham, 77–79, 177
Attorney general, 26–27
Audit, 101–2

Baker v. *Carr*, 146
Barber, James David, 11–12, 174
Barnard, C. I., 178
Bills: drafting of, 48–50, 84; final passage of, 55–56, 87
Buffering, 3–4, 25, 27, 43, 46–47, 52, 55, 175

Cohesion, 15–16
Committees, 29–40, 149–50; action by, 84–86; Committee of the Whole, 30, 149; conference committees, 32, 37, 56–57, 87–88; hearings by, 51, 52; interim committees, 4, 30, 32, 33–35; Post Audit Committee, 68–71; Rules Committee, 177; screening function of, 51–53; standing committees, 30; Ways and Means Committee, 64–66
Complexity, 148
Concepts, 1–6

Derthick, Martha, 68, 177
Dill, William R., 174
Diversity, 148
Docking, Robert, 65, 92
Dye, Thomas, 176

Easton, David, 44, 175
Educational expenditures, 141
Employees, 8–10
Employment, 142
Environmental changes, 163
Executive-branch agencies, 23

Federal grants, 143
Federal Home Owners Corporation, 156
Federalist 51, 137
Fiscal review, 64–67, 88–89
Froman, Lewis A., Jr., 173, 176

General orders, 53–55, 86–87
Governor, 23, 45, 57, 88
Greenstein, Fred I., 177

Harder, Marvin, 24, 174
Harris News Service, 25
Huntington, Samuel, 138, 148

Informal groups, 40

Institutional imperatives, 4–5
Institutionalization, 148–61
Institutions, 4–5
Interest groups, 24–25

Jewell, Malcolm, 173
Judges, 26

Kansas City Star and *Times*, 25
Kansas Department of Economic De-
velopment, 173
Kansas Social Welfare Act, 142
Keefe, William J., 173

Leadership, 81–93
Legis 50, 166–67
Legislative Administrative Services, 10,
17, 102–5
Legislative Budget Committee, 97
Legislative Coordinating Council, 96, 97
Legislative Council, 92–93, 96, 153–56,
158
Legislative Counsel, 10, 158–59
Legislative Post Audit, 9, 17, 68–71, 99–
102, 105–8, 160, 170
Legislative Post Audit, Division of, 96,
157–58
Legislative Postsecondary Educational
Planning Committee (1202 Commis-
sion), 97
Legislative Reference, 159
Legislative Research Department, 9, 17,
96–99, 105–8, 149, 155–57
Legislative staff organizations, 95
Legislative turnover, 151–52
Legislators, 8, 9, 11–16, 20–21
Legislatures, 7, 58–60
Loux, Richard, 92

McGill, Duane S., 92–93
Madison, James, 137
March, James G., 176
Mayhew, David R., 176
Media, 25–26
Montesqieu, 62–63

Nadel, Mark V., 177
Neumann, Franz, 177

Neutral competence, 18–19
NIRA, 156

Occupations of Kansas legislators, 16
Ogul, Morris, 79, 173, 177
Organization theory, 2
Overseeing, 61–80

Patronage, 20, 92
Patterson, Samuel, 173
Political institutions, 138, 170
Political organizations, 138, 170
Political parties, 40, 57
Polsby, Nelson, 148, 177
Population, 139–40
Prager, David, 174, 177
Pressman, Jeffrey, 176
Presthus, Robert, 12, 174
Professionals, 18–19, 96

Rampey, Carolyn, 24, 174
Retainers, 20–21
Revisor of Statutes, 9, 17, 149, 154–55
Rourke, Francis, 177
Rules and regulations, 67–68, 89–90

School Foundation Finance Act, 140
Secretaries and clerks, 19–20
Selznick, Philip, 5, 173, 178
Seniority system, 32
Serrano v. *Preist*, 146
Simon, Herbert A., 176
Smith, Glee, 93
Social Security Act of 1935, 145
Specialization, 8–27
State employees, 147
State Finance Council, 26, 71, 74–76
State Library, 159
*State of Kansas, ex rel., Curt T. Schnei-
der, Attorney General,* v. *Robert
Bennett, Governor of the State of
Kansas, et al., 1977,* 26
State Printing Office, 104
Supreme Court, 26–27

Task environment, 2–3, 21–27
Technology, 3, 41–60, 95, 149, 170
Thompson, Frank, 163–64